THE LAW OF POSITIVE THINKING

-A SUCCESS GUIDE FOR TEENS AND YOUNG ADULTS

RAJ D.RAJPAL

PIONEER COMMUNICATION

PIONEER COMMUNICATION
BOOK SHOWCASE

FINANCE SERIES
OFFSHORE INVESTMENTS: THE MILLIONAIRE VISION
OFFSHORE HAVENS: THE FOUR BEST-KEPT SECRETS OF MILLIONAIRES
QUANTUM CRISIS 1
QUANTUM CRISIS 2
QUANTUM CRISIS 3
QUANTUM CRISIS 4

SALES AND MARKETING SERIES
QUANTUM SELLING
QUANTUM SALES MANAGEMENT
QUANTUM MARKETING

MANAGEMENT SERIES
QUANTUM ETHICS

SELF-IMPROVEMENT SERIES
QUANTUM PUBLIC SPEAKING
POSITIVE THINKING FOR TEENAGERS
POSITIVE THINKING FOR ADULTS

SPIRITUALITY/NEW AGE SERIES
YOU HAVE IT ALL NOW: YOUR LIFE IS TRULY
YOURS TO DISCOVER & ENJOY
UNCONDITIONAL LOVE
BEYOND THE MIND
TOWARDS THE UNKNOWN

OTHER FORTHCOMING BOOKS
UNCONDITIONAL YOGA
UNCONDITIONAL HEALTH
UNCONDITIONAL WEALTH
UNCONDITIONAL SUCCESS
UNCONDITIONAL HEALING
UNCONDITIONAL SPIRITUALITY
UNCONDITIONAL WEIGHT LOSS

THE LAW OF POSITIVE THINKING

-A SUCCESS GUIDE FOR TEENS AND YOUNG ADULTS

RAJ D. RAJPAL

B.Sc.(Honors), D.A.P.R., D.M., D.C.S., D.P.S., M.B.A.(Ohio)

Sales Coach and Public Speaker
Canadian National Quality Award Winner
Trainer, Bob Proctor Basic Program, Canada
Magna cum Laude, MBA Program, Ohio, U.S.A.
Sales Trainer, Counselor Selling Program, U.S.A.
Trophy Winner, Public Speaking, Indo-American Society
Provisional Applicant, Million Dollar Round Table, U.S.A.
Diploma, Graduate Advertising & Public Relations Program.
Trainer, Bob Proctor Advanced Motivation Series Program, Canada
Uni-Lever Gold Medal Recipient-Graduate Marketing Management Program

PIONEER COMMUNICATION

PUBLISHER :
PIONEER COMMUNICATION, CANADA

Orders for additional books can be placed directly at:
Pioneercommunication1@yahoo.com
(Sales Discounts on multiple copy orders)

National Library of Canada
Rajpal Raj D., 1951-
Positive Thinking for Teenagers/Raj D. Rajpal
ISBN : 978-0-9783550-6-7
Copyright 2015 Raj D.Rajpal ALL RIGHTS RESERVED

This book is dedicated to the growth, nurturing and development of teenagers, who exist in a challenging and volatile home, family and peer group environment. This book is written with the hope and prayer that teenagers learn and adapt and be cognizant of what it will take to succeed and be happy in the twenty first century.

A keen awareness of all factors in the environment, both positive and negative and the ability to change their mental, emotional and spiritual traits to achieve lasting success is the main mission of this book.

May it be a small but growing light of wisdom and intelligence in its contribution to the success of our young citizens. May it afford them an opportunity to succeed in whatever they choose to become in a spirit of ease and happiness.

A special prayer for my daughter, Natasha, who may grow meaningfully and positively as she faces the challenges of adulthood and grows and matures into a beautiful lotus flower!!!!!!

TABLE OF CONTENTS

INTRODUCTION

Teenagers are the future of Civilization as we understand ---- the values, concepts and principles they imbibe form the wellspring of their behavior in the future. Therefore, it is most important to understand these "valuable" human beings, to get a feel of the environmental and cultural conditions in which they are raised and then understand how these imbibed values and traditions affect their day to day Life with its resultant impact on their Societies and World Conditions at large.

When viewed at a Macrocosmic level, such teenage behavior does not only affect the Life of an individual Nation but also deeply affects the way Nations look across the ocean to each other and interact to each other's differing ways of thinking, philosophizing and view of Life and Living. This perception, in turn, affects their attitude and resultant action, which culminates in either dominance and violence or caring and openness to each other. This then, affects the future creation of Wars or better still an alternative World view, one which allows people, nations and human beings to attempt to explore the possibility of living together in Peace and Co-operation.

Positive thinking forms the first step in understanding and expressing human behavior. And a good spirit involved with the expression and implementation of positive thinking in teenagers marks one of the first steps in providing opportunity to youngsters to live a happy, peaceful and productive Life and develop the skills to financially and emotionally succeed while developing a capacity to interact with different cultures and value systems (amicably). The alternate is War, Violence and Division by Psychological (Mental) walls----- something no one really wants.

This book attempts to give youngsters a Roadmap to understand themselves better and also help them deal with their relationships with parents, peer groups, and institutions.

Life is all about Relationships, so the book is structured in Chapter form, concentrating study in each chapter to an understanding of one specific relationship between Positive Thinking and a specific subject area. The hope is that by reading and understanding all these different relationships, a teenager can not only cope with all the volatility and uncertainty surrounding the growing years, but also come up with a smart, practical, hands on solution to making Life more meaningful, worthwhile and productive.

With this newfound understanding, a teenager should be able to figure out the best career for his future, understand his inherent strengths and weaknesses and stay away from distractions and energy robbing schemes, which most definitely will undermine his future Career, Business and Happiness.

The choice is the teenager's: live a Life of distraction, abuse, and over-involvement in sex and other trivial pursuits or create and maintain a Life of Meaning and Value. This book tries to clarify and demonstrate the Value and Significance of a Life well lived as seen through the eyes of a teenager.

And it starts and ends with a hypothesis that all Values need to be understood, learnt and applied by such teenager. In the process, a Parent and a Teenager both share initial responsibility for this knowledge and education. Later on, the responsibility shifts completely to a teenager. This book is an entertaining, yet serious ride through Teenage Life and the importance of Positive Thinking in it.

So many young lives have been lost to drugs, alcohol and premature sex--- it is the author's hope and prayer that this book marks a beginning to a more meaningful and happy Life for all young teenagers.

Positive thinking does make a sea change in the way Life is perceived. The Law of Attraction has undeniable and irrefutable proof that you become what you think and/or what you fear/do not believe in. You attract your visualized abundance or your fear of failure. If youngsters learn this vital fact, then they will engage in positive thought and action 100% of the time. And if they change their attitude and behavior they will learn to move mountains; they will also learn to help others and grow in a spirit of joy, co-operation and mutual success.

And is that not the Meaning of Life? Superlative contribution to Society, a caring and concern for others, an identification of a career which is right for a youngster and the courage to set high goals and believe they are achievable.

This book tries to exemplify such values by providing an effective Road Map for teenagers to achieve whatever they wish----- in Essence, living a Life without limitations accompanied with Maximum Success and Performance.

MISSION STATEMENT

This book has multiple missions. Let us look at each of them and then try to integrate all the objectives governing the writing of this book.

The first mission is to educate a teenager, who has been thrust into this world with massive cultural, religious and peer pressure conditioning. This teenager, in order to get out of this conditioned "rut", needs to look beyond. How does one look into the present and future with all the burdens of the past??? One effective way is to develop skills and knowledge and use these in a positive spirit with a view to succeeding in Life and reaching whatever peak one chooses to reach. One great North American contribution to the world is its undaunted spirit, its great sense of courage and its ability to empower its citizens to take risks with a view to capturing a dream. These are the very qualities required from teenagers as they seek to build a better future, undaunted by all the negative conditioning surrounding them.

The second mission of the book, closely related to the first is to teach teenagers the essentials of the Law of Attraction. How many young teenagers are encouraged to dream big? How many teenagers understand, accept and implement the fact that they can attract anything they wish by focusing on that wish dominantly? Also, that the power of positive intent always manifests itself in their reality. How many of these children have attended a "Power of Attraction" workshop and are engaged in public and private discussions on this important Law of Action? The Law of Attraction is a very vital way of bringing dreams come true and what better way to encourage teenagers than to teach them how to apply the Law of Attraction to get what they want, while respecting the right of others to live and express themselves, accompanied with a spirit of Love and Reverence?

The third mission of the book is to teach teenagers the essential laws regarding goal setting, visualization and career planning. Such skills will assist them grow in their respective careers and business while maintaining a healthy physical, emotional, mental and spiritual Psyche.

The fourth mission of the book is to make available to the teenager, the creation of "dynamite energy", which generates itself by application of the Laws of Spirituality. This is gained by accessing the most fundamental source of Universal Energy through Prayer, Meditation and Intentional Focus.

The fifth mission of the book is to explore the circle of 32 relationships as such relationships interrelate and interact---- we are now discussing specific relationships between positive thinking and a specific area of teenage Life. Why are these 32 circles important?

Because these 32 circles form the basis of Teenage Success or Failure. This book expands each circle of relationship in detail and in the Book Summary links all 32 circles together to form an integrated, comprehensive understanding of the qualities teenagers need to achieve lasting Success in their Life.

These five missions are all closely related since one cannot function effectively without the other (for optimal Success). The missions are defined as follows:

Book Mission 1: To create the necessary skills and habits to succeed in School and in your Career.

Book Mission 2: To learn, accept and apply the Principles of the Law of Attraction

Book Mission 3: To learn the essentials of goal setting and visualization and to successfully apply them in your Life.

Book Mission 4: To connect with Universal Reality through application of the Laws of Spirituality.

Book Mission 5: To understand Life is a Circle and essentially composed of relationships and the understanding, application of the circle of 32 relationships as they relate to achieving an uncommon dream.

Why is the author propounding again these five basic mission statements? Because, on close examination, one can see they are all connected into a Universal Whole. Integrating good skills and habits, setting realistic goals within well defined time frameworks, using the Law of Attraction to motivate yourself to achieve such goals, using principles of the Spiritual Laws to make it easy and stress-free to get to where you want to go by unlocking a flood of Energy and integrating all 32 circles of relationship all work together to create a better and more successful Teenager. Integration of all these various facts, concepts and principles working comprehensively and smoothly together assist in making your 'Life-engine' work at peak performance. This now becomes a pathway to successful, yet stress free Living.

I hope and pray you enjoy this practical and lucid presentation. Most importantly, **the author wishes that a careful study of this book, leads to a personal transformation of the teenage Life in a way which encourages Excellence, Happiness and Peak Performance**.

The author urges every parent to take the initial responsibility of assisting their own child in being the best they can be in the field of academic study, sports, goal setting, individual achievement, appropriate career selection and ultimately in the selfless service to others.

Best wishes, my teenage friend, as you discover new Pathways to Success.

Let the light of Universal Energy be your friend and ally as you marshal your Energy to reach even higher levels of Success in School, Friendship, Career and Future Life.

CHAPTER 1

POSITIVE THINKING AND SUCCESS

Years back, I was rendered a brilliant definition of Success. In this definition, Success was defined as "the realization of a pre-determined worthwhile goal." What better definition of Success can one come up with, which in a miracle sentence describes what Success is all about?

Now let us understand this definition in its application to teenagers. Does the teenage mind understand what Success is? And where does he get his inspiration in determining what is and what isn't a worthwhile goal? And how does he predetermine his disposition towards an understanding of Success? To start with an understanding of Success, a young teenage Mind needs to examine the overall value of a goal. Is the goal he has set accomplishing a worthwhile Social, Family, Career, Educational or other relevant cause? The teenage must decide for himself what is relevant or what is irrelevant, but the thinking to filter the "value causes" from the irrelevant "pseudo causes" and the training to know the difference is vital for the young mind. Parents and educational institutions must inculcate this level of rationality in their children and encourage them to make the right decisions for themselves----- however, the right decisions are not what the parents want from their kids but what the kids feel most happy doing in their natural environment. Teenagers normally draw their inspiration from their family, social and religious environment.

What is most important is to allow the young mind to explore different areas of career pursuit; accompanied with a spirit of exploration and experimentation, it should not be very difficult for a young person to identify two or three worthwhile career choices for his shortlist of future possibility. What is really critical is to encourage the teenager to choose his options on his own and to encourage him to pursue what he enjoys most. Because it has been proven again and again, that unless a person does what he enjoys most, Success will be but a fleeting experience. And alas, so many kids get attracted to fleeting Success. And this type of Success is exactly the opposite of what is required; one needs to get into a Calling or Profession, which will last for a lifetime and allow the young teenager to work through the ups and downs of his career and stay focused till Success is within his grasp.

Positive thinking is a great aid to teenage success if understood and applied properly in the achievement of his predetermined, worthwhile goal. So predetermination is the process which the teenage decides on in terms of identifying any worthwhile goal (like a career goal). As he moves forward to achieve this goal, it naturally becomes precious and worthwhile, because he has chosen it.

But is making money and succeeding in a Career or Business the only definition of Success? This is where Society and Parents have failed these young "diamonds in the rough".

As a young teenager goes through his Life, a lot more is required for him to succeed as his Environment is constantly feeding him definitions of Success as being purely material---- unfortunately, the best definitions and raison-de-etre of Success is missing if we look at Success is only being a material achievement.

A teenager must be encouraged to cultivate a World view to really be successful, long-term. And this view must necessarily be different than the way in which he is being conditioned through his immediate environment. For a lot of North American kids, a definition of Success surrounds being loved by their parents, by doing modestly well in School, possessing a girlfriend and being accepted by his peer group. But Life is a lot vaster and significant than that and just these values, some of which may be important and valuable like being loved by their parents misses the big picture.

The bigger picture of Success is one's seamless and happy connection with the World and a purpose in Life, which calls for the service of others, while engaging in work which is truly satisfying. So, for a teenager, I would challenge him to look at the World in the following way:

I am one of about 7 billion inhabitants, who share what we know as "Mother Earth". Do you feel pretty insignificant? You should not. You need to adopt a spiritual view, which says out loud and clear the following message: "I have been endowed by a divine quality, which makes me unique in every way, because there is only one of me (with these exact psychological qualities in the World). Being unique and yet one among many people who share this World and Space, I am humble and strive to maintain a positive stance towards all beings and creatures around me, both in my immediate space and those who live in different cultures beyond my ocean and reach.

So, the first quality, which will take you far in your Life, is a spirit of Humility.

Secondly, your uniqueness also means that you have certain God-given strengths and inherent weaknesses and flaws and that you choose to live Life focusing and building on your strengths and ignoring your weaknesses.

Thirdly, you look at Success as a broad based result in many different areas of your Life, which includes your relationship with your parents, your relationship with your friends, your relationship with your place of learning and all who assist you there and your relationship with the immediate world at large. You also choose to excel in your relationship to your body (Health), your relationship to your Mind (attitude, actions and behavior) and your relationship with the Universal Energy (Spirituality) and your relationship with your heart (Emotions).

When we discuss Success as achievement of a predetermined worthwhile goal, let us now amplify this definition to include your achievement in all the following areas:

1. Your relationship with your parents.
2. Your relationship with your friends.
3. Your relationship with your educational institutions.
4. Your relationship with the World at large.
5. Your relationship with your goals.
6. Your relationship with your image of your future Career.
7. Your relationship with your ideas.
8. Your relationship with your body (Health).
9. Your relationship with your Mind (Values, Principles), Higher Energy (Spirituality) and your Emotions (Feelings).

Therefore, Success becomes the everlasting quest to hit consistently, a multi-dimensional moving target. The process of achievement involves active and alert participation in determining where you are now and where you want to go in the future. Positive thinking accelerates the achievement of your goal, as you undertake this journey to reach your destination. Faith, conviction, courage when accompanied with enthusiasm and self-determination make this journey even more fun and fulfilling. Because it is the journey we must enjoy before we realize the fruits of our dreams. Positive thinking is the elixir which keeps you "high" on this road trip and allows you to weather the storms, which inevitably must appear before you reach your prize at the end of the rainbow. And yes, the pot of gold is there to be claimed by those individuals who harness all their mental, emotional and spiritual power through use of Positive Thinking.

CHAPTER 2

POSITIVE THINKING AND SEX

One of the early challenges faced by a teenager is the preponderance of ideas, feelings and real and imagined experiences relating to Sex. It is a well known and accepted fact that there are two forms of Energy in the World, a masculine energy and a feminine energy. However, unknown to most people, both these sources of Energy reside in each individual in varying proportions; a man may have a greater disposition of female energy which makes him act in a way others consider as "effeminate." A woman may have extreme masculine qualities like aggression, which label her as something more masculine. On a subtler level there are physical energy attraction centers, with the male energy being drawn to a physical counterpart (female energy).

Coming back to the life of a teenager in North America, the urge to express oneself sexually accelerates as he matures through teenage years. A lot of this pressure comes from peer sources; a teenage student is considered to be abnormal if he does not have a girlfriend by a certain age and once he acquires a girlfriend, the question of a sexual relationship starts in his mind. Peer pressure automatically equates acquisition of a girlfriend with possession of a sexual relationship.

I am not here to profess the merits or demerits of a sexual relationship in teenagers. What I need to express is the fact that the use of Sexual Energy at an early age creates a lot of hindrances for the teenager. As a young person grows and expresses oneself, he requires all the Energy he can muster to study, engage in sports, choose a career path and adjust to the constantly changing scope of his environment. Sex at an early age creates a major energy drag and distraction. It descends a teenager into a realm of experience most aptly reserved for mature adult Life. For what is a teenager to know about love and how easy is it to mix the essence of Love with lust, which accompanies a physical relationship?

But who is going to teach this teenager the difference? Looking around North America, I feel the young teenager has been left to fend for himself in terms of his views on sexuality and his role models around him have terribly failed in helping him understand Reality, which educates him on the fundamental difference between Love accompanied with Sex and only a Sexual experience. It is quite natural for a teenager to want to explore his physical aspect and its relationship with his counterpart, the female aspect. But alas, this is not the time for such exploration, even though his hormones may be activated.

The critical advice I can give teenagers is this:

First, you have your entire Life ahead to experience Sexual matters. This is definitely not the right time and place to do it. These years of growth and transformation from your teenage years to adulthood are crucial. You do have a choice, however hard it may be.

You can choose to go against the mainstream of peer pressure and have good friendships with females, knowing that Sex is not crucial to your enjoyment of your female counterpart. What is the benefit of having friendships without Sex through your teen years?

In my mind, there are numerous benefits. Let me enumerate them:

1. The ability to gather your available energy and focus on your studies and career work.
2. The ability to stay more balanced "emotionally."
3. The power not to be distracted energy wise from improper or disastrous sexual encounters, which must follow at some point or another if you choose to engage in this behavior at an early age.
4. A lopsided and imperfect view of the female role model. Women are meant to be appreciated, respected and adored. They have marvelous qualities and there is also a time and place for Sex. The time is just not right now.
5. The ability to sharpen your sports and intellectual/study skills.
6. The opportunity to have ALL your energy available to search, seek, explore, experiment with your future career choices.
7. An opportunity to prevent you from engaging in fatherhood at an early stage of your Life and losing your focus. For a woman there is the additional challenging emotional and physical situation when she has an unplanned emergency. For such woman, this pregnancy could spell disaster for her Future. North America has hundreds of thousands of single parent mothers, whose partners have abandoned them for one reason or another and these mothers are forced to fend for themselves and their babies. Their goes the farm!!! Instead of having the opportunity to study, grow and mature, the female is forced to radically alter her Life and loses an opportunity to grow into an independent person financially and is thrust forcefully into poverty as she struggles to survive with her new born infant. She also loses the chance to meet the right partner and have a beautiful married Life later. In short, your whole Life goes down the toilet for the participation in one or more unplanned sexual acts. Is this what your Life was meant to create for you? I do not think so, since every woman deserves to live Life to the fullest with maximum opportunity to enjoy, express and relate to others in a spirit of joy.
8. An opportunity to allow mental rationality to rule over your emotions at the early stages of teen hood, making it considerably easier for you to stay on edge and live a balanced Life overall.

The choice is finally yours: live like your peer group, get wasted, indulge in alcohol clandestinely, have numerous sexual relationships, lose your edge and focus in over-involvement with the female person or alternatively choose to live comfortably, sanely, stay on edge and focused in your Life and be free of any one person's needs and domination and demand.

Positive thinking in its relationship with Sex, can assist a person explore his innate abilities and conceptualize a better Life. Initially, this may be difficult as a teenager watches all his friends hook up with someone or the other. Social situations can also be somewhat clumsy and awkward when teenagers entertain in pairs and as a teenager, you may feel uncomfortable (going alone) in such social situations. However, if you focus positively on the benefits of a celibate, non-sexual Life in your teens and understand how such behavior impacts positively your future advancement, your sharp edged focus, your balance and most importantly your personal freedom, you can realize you can have as many female friends as you wish and even have a girlfriend----- but you do not allow sexual situations (currently or potentially) to distract you from all the other good things you want to do in Life, like travel, meet new people, learn new things and excel in your Studies, moving that much closer in achieving your lifelong dreams of self-reliance, including career formation and maturity.

Life is wonderful: the challenge to live non-sexually in teenage Life invariably throws up massive benefits. In short, the benefits of this way of Life far exceeds the costs of abstinence. Now each teenager needs to decide for himself which way to go. Go mainstream like your peers and eventually suffer and mal-adjust or go off stream and live a better, more valuable and meaningful Life.

CHAPTER 3

POSITIVE THINKING & HEALTH, SPORTS & PHYSICAL ACTIVITY

One of the crucial elements critical to teenage success is good health accompanied with optimum sports and physical activity. A teenager has particular needs as he is growing. His body is maturing and expanding and requires a healthy balance of nutrition, sports and physical activity, which then impact his overall health.

As he grows, his parents need to pay close attention to how he is developing health wise------ is he prone to disease or any physical vulnerabilities? Should special attention be paid to any areas of his physique, which require extra attention? How is his food eating habit? Does he eat regularly? Does he follow the food chart religiously? Or is his eating haphazard and skewed towards a more calorie and carbohydrate intensive diet? Is he obese?

A teenager, if smart and intelligent, can take charge of his health and take full responsibility for achieving a high energy level. The critical part here is his motivation to achieve quantifiable physical goals; when he looks around at his classroom situated, say, somewhere in North America, he typically sees a large section of students with moderate to intense obesity. He also sees his classmates eating junk food, drinking a great deal of soda and in general having bad nutrition habits. What can be the motivation behind being different than the crowd? The goal setting process is really important at this age. Parents can assist teenagers set realistic and achievable goals. But what is the wellspring of action? Parents can instill the positive rewards of creating and maintaining health centric behavior. Some rewards could be:

1. Having a strong and healthy physique.
2. Being more attractive and acceptable to the opposite sex helping him forge happy emotional relationships.
3. Being healthy can be associated with more energy to achieve the student dreams of maximal success in the classroom and in other cu-curricular pursuits (as a result of being able to exploit a higher energy source).
4. Being a leader and role model to other students through using his energy to participate and excel in sports and other physical activities.
5. Living a disease free Life, which creates the time and energy space to create and maintain happy friendships and afford an opportunity to travel as well as excel in study.

A persistent and continual positive thinking process assists the teenager reach his health goals easier and better. However, positive thinking does not exist in a vacuum. For positive thinking to be effective, it must be combined with a motivational drive. Nothing assists the inner motivation more than the rewards associated with a modified behavior (as compared to peer activity) and this reward structure must be accompanied by the written commitment to clear and identifiable goals and a definite plan of action (to achieve such health goals).

In terms of positive thinking and its effect on health, a parent must instill on a teenager the definition of "good health." Health is not only physical performance but also includes mental and emotional wellbeing. Setting goals for mental and emotional health are more challenging but are essential for a complete well rounded application of positive thinking.

The teenager, if advanced and independent, could ask himself what makes him feel intellectually well balanced (mental) and again, what makes him happy (emotional). In addition he must clarify and crystallize what makes him feel a sense of accomplishment (mental) and also what turns him on in physical activity (emotional). Once these needs, desires and inclinations are put in writing, goals to achieve those outcomes can be set. The teenager needs, desires and inclinations become the turning point, which motivate the accomplishment of intellectual and emotional goals for better Health. So, positive thinking accompanied with goal setting, reward structure definition and a definite plan of action for all aspects of Health, including mental, emotional and physical health provide the best future arrangement for the accomplishment of all Health goals.

POSITIVE THINKING AND ITS ROLE IN ACHIEVEMENT OF TEENAGE SPORTS GOALS.

A teenager needs to express his energy in various physical paths. Sports are a very important in his physical development process. The field of Sports teaches the value of team play and Leadership; it also guides one in excelling in things other than study and it is also a very good distracting counterbalancing force to Study.

The teenager needs to identify which sport he enjoys most and then put his efforts there. It has always been found that a person will excel in what he loves most and parents should be careful not to force a certain sport on a child.

Now how can a teenager use the art of positive thinking for sports success? The law of attraction, which will be covered in a special chapter shows how this law can be used, combined with positive thinking to create lasting achievement in the field of sport. Positive thinking shows a teenager how to dream big, how to compete effectively, how to harness the power of team play to reach a common goal and creates the strength and energy to move on to make his team and/or himself an outstanding player.

In the process, positive thinking aids him in visualization and achievement of his goals, develops his enthusiasm and gives him that gush of energy which accompanies a positive outcome on the field.

POSITIVE THINKING AND ITS ROLE IN DETERMINATION OF OPTIMAL PHYSICAL ACTIVITY.

As the teenage grows and develops, he exhibits strong physical activity. The challenge here is to temper the physical activity with periods of rest. Not to forget periods of introspection and time devoted to the impartial understanding of the environment around him. The key here is balance; so many teenagers are so caught up in their physical environment that they lose sight of the bigger picture.

A teenager needs to balance his physical energy demands with well planned rest periods and some quiet and relaxing time, including periods set aside for prayer and meditation. Yoga also assists in this process to relax and de-stress a young active person. Positive thinking can help create an important sense of balance for the teenager as he juggles between all the various demands on his time and energy. A successful teenager is a balanced teenager and Positive thinking helps a teenager become more aware of the time he spends on different activities in a day. This in turn helps him analyze where he is using his time productively and where he is engaging in wasteful activity, which in turn assists in the modification of his activities to ensure better result accomplishment, accompanied with more fun and less stress... When positive thinking is combined with effective time management the teenager becomes much more aware of how he is utilizing his energy and by analyzing his activity at the end of every day, he can determine if he is moving in the right direction or not.

CHAPTER 4

POSITIVE THINKING AND FAMILY ENVIRONMENT

Teenagers are greatly influenced by their family environment. In fact, cultural and family conditioning colors the eyes of a young person. Which part of the world you were born in, the religious orientation of your parents, the socio-economic achievement of your family and the deep expressed and unexpressed values of your family create either a motivating or a backward lash in your future teenage Life.

And how is such a teenager to separate himself from the omnipotent influence of his family? What if he is brainwashed with the wrong values, which hold him in poor stead as he plans to climb the ladder of success? Study after study in North America show a great correlation between parent and child success. If one is brought up in a neurotic, schizophrenic environment, then those parental qualities get sub-consciously imbibed in a young teenager. They color his Life and his future success or failure. And what obviously follows this influence is years and years of frustration where a talented teenager cannot exceed his own expectations, due to poor family upbringing. The wrong inherited values of poverty, negativism and poor self-esteem come in the way of such teenager's success.

The law of attraction, combined with positive thinking energy, is one way of overcoming this very major obstacle to teenage success. But who is to educate the teenager? His deranged or backward looking parents? A poor educational system? His teachers? His friends? In many instances, it is the teenager himself, who creates the conditions to step out of poverty and faulty thinking patterns inherited through his family and environmental background. This teenager realizes something is wrong in the results he is achieving and he believes he deserves more from his Life. This feeling of frustration then creates a positive motivating path for the teenager. He is then motivated to find better and creative ways to reach success.

Other issues like lack of self-esteem and lack of quality education are more challenging factors to overcome, particularly where teenagers have been indoctrinated with such negative values and conditioning in their family environment.

The author really hopes that more "centers of educational excellence" spring up over the world to empower these misdirected teenagers; alas there has not been much progress in this area, to date.

Several prescriptions can be provided to overcome a "negative-valued" family environment. Some of these recommendations are:

1. Profuse reading. A teenager should be encouraged to read as much as possible and not only fictional books, but works of art and nonfiction and business, science and history books. The more reading diversity, the greater the breadth of knowledge exposure, which will improve his practical perceptions and understanding.
2. Some exposure to the field of Motivation Science and Sales training. Good books, audiotapes, mp3, and training videos and cd's will help.
3. Study of the Law of Attraction would be most advantageous in making the teenage mind believe that he can accomplish anything he wants, provided he focuses on such outcome constantly and consistently.
4. Attendance at motivation seminars would be very beneficial.
5. Joining a teenage motivation club through the internet, would be a great way to interact with other teenagers all over the world.
6. Selection of successful role models in fields of work most close to the aspiration of a teenager would help him visualize that he, too, could reach that level of future success.

Positive thinking can play a great role in the acceleration of success for a teenager as he learns to overcome his own and his inherited negative tendency. Positive thinking will reassure the teenager that his Life and Mind is his own and that he can choose whatever thoughts he wishes. And this type of approach will bless him with an understanding that positive thinking is the only key, which will allow him to step out of his family environment and conditioning into a better world colored by his own positive thoughts and actions.

However, this process of Change is very challenging and teenagers need to gather that raw spirit of aggression and hunger so that they can motivate themselves to lead a more worthwhile and productive Life----- a Life, which is blessed by both economic success and an enduring sense of Happiness.

CHAPTER 5

POSITIVE THINKING AND RELIGION/FAITH/CONDITIONING

Religion and Faith form the foundation for a good, Happy and Success Life. Conditioning on the other hand is the antithesis of beauty and achievement. The teenage mind needs to be impressed of how these forces work against each other. It is very much like the biblical description of good and evil. Good is represented by positive spirituality and faith, while conditioning represents the evil in our Life.

Why is religion and faith important for a teenager? And why should this teenager try to understand the great impact religion and faith have in his Life? When I discuss religion I mean, " Spirituality," which is a concept beyond the traditional understanding of religion-----it is a way of Living one's Life, in which all actions, thoughts and behavior result in men living freely and happily without imposing violence, pain and domination on each other. Spirituality is an understanding and reverence of Life itself and of all living creatures inhabiting our Mother Earth. Does this sound like indoctrination class in Spirituality? Absolutely not.

If more kids were taught the basic Principles of Spirituality like loving and respecting their neighbor and understanding and following the Ten Commandments, Life would be much better on Mother Earth.

Faith is the elixir of Life----- it is the miraculous element which spurs creativity, love and everlasting success.

In normal teenage life, both Spirituality and Faith appear to be missing in major proportion. Life, even for a teenager, becomes an unconscious struggle to achieve and adulate more and more material success and teenagers only have their "eyes and ears" cocked up when it comes to any matter involving someone acquiring a bigger house, more money in the bank, a more fun electronic toy and fancier clothes. Faith, on the other hand, is missing totally unless one is blessed to be either born in an intelligent, sensitive faith-oriented family or if a teenager is blessed with a God-given individual capacity, motivation and intelligence to transcend conditionings and other inherited limitations.

How does one inculcate a spirit of Spirituality in a young teenager? By allowing them exposure to new thoughts, ideas and feelings without any prejudgment. By allowing such teenager a free rein to experiment with new projects, whether such project involves Yoga, Meditation or any other esoteric calling. Teenagers need to experiment to understand how the other half of the world lives and nothing is more educational than taking a risk through experimentation. Another eye opener to open up an "inner spiritual center" for a teenager is to allow him to travel to a developing third world country.

This travel will create a real sense of appreciation on this young person's part, as he may realize that he is far better off than many of his counterpart humans all over the world. It will also create a keener sense of sensitivity and tolerance to people from different worlds and walks of Life. This may lessen his cravings for merely material things and make him search for value in other endeavors and pursuits.

Conditioning is very negative. Let me explain what I mean by conditioning.

Conditioning is an "unconsciously" forced, pre-determined way of looking at any situation outside you. It is usually taught through your parents, your culture and your peer group. To be free from conditioning, one has to be first aware of its existence. Only after you realize you have so many biased, unproven values and concepts that you open up to the possibility of change. And change is essential for better Living. For a teenager this may be hard to envision. He is used to his routine, his friends, his school and his set way of doing things in his environment. Why should such teenage want to go through the pain and pressure of effecting change in his Life?

Here are some reasons for consideration of change:

1. Life is full of adventure and excitement and being aware of your values, inherited or learned will assist you in becoming better by overcoming flaws and perfecting your strengths. This is done by readjusting/discarding poor values and replacing them with more positive learning experiences.

2. Successful teenagers love to experiment with new ideas for fun. Why not try to look at what you are doing in a different way? Can you do something better by changing the way you do it? Also, if you saw any flaws you have inherited or assumed and saw that by correcting them you would have a more fun and happier/more successful life, would you make the changes to reach this more positive result?

3. You are a unique teenager and there is only one of you in this world. Do you want to help others live a better and more satisfying Life? Do you realize that before you can help anyone else you have to help yourself? Why not start this process by looking at you from the inside out, on a non-judgmental basis. Understand the real you and then, you will make a difference not only in your life but also in another's life.

4. Do you like to have fun? Why not study your friend's traits? Try to identify what are the dominant inherited traits and conditioned and unconscious values and tendencies. And make your friend do the same thing to you. Then see if you agree with each other's assessments. If not, get a third friend involved and study his comments.

Giving teenagers fun ways to experiment and grow, will provide a motivation for a lasting change and give them a chance to overcome any lack of spirituality and faith and eliminate some major conditionings so that their mind is free to learn and explore a better way to live.

A life of positive thought and action emphasizes there is hope for a better tomorrow. It helps you understand your spirituality and faith and helps you accentuate these qualities and understanding. Positive thinking, when accompanied with ever-eternal awareness also assists in discovering your flaws and weak spots acquired with hereditary and environmental conditioning and helps provide a smooth way forward to more Success, both economically and in the pursuit of inner happiness and satisfaction.

CHAPTER 6

POSITIVE THINKING AND ACADEMIC STUDY

Academic study forms the first part of the growing years of a teenager---- it is an ideal preparation point into the future world of work and business (for a teenager). The role of school education is to prepare a child to assume and enjoy the responsibilities of adulthood. A major part of this responsibility is in assisting a teenager isolate the right career for himself, one in which he is both happy and can serve others excellently. Therefore, education must provide the right resources and environment for the flourishing of a human mind. Alas, this condition is not true since most schools either emphasize exclusively a high level of academic achievement or a mundane curriculum. In numerous situations all over the world, schools have failed tremendously in their responsibility of nurturing a creative and integrated Mind. Therefore, in most instances, the teenager turns to his parent(s) to assist him learn and grow. In this regard, it becomes a parent's responsibility to educate the child to develop not only the skills associated with Mathematics and Science, but also the right outlook to Life. And what if, the parent himself is not educated in a holistic, integrated manner? If the parent attended a poor public school, what kind of educational values can he expect to impart a child since his value and educational system may not help the child get to where he wants to go in the future?

This poses a real challenge to the teenager. The young teenager needs to take charge and assume responsibility for his future. Look around you and one can notice different shades of adult characters and personality derived through a myriad of educational systems. The key for a teenager is to focus on his needs, wants and desires and make a sincere effort to know where he wants to be in the future and then marshal "teenage resources" to get there. Do not forget for a second how important education is for your future success. Research after research has proven that college graduates earn substantially more in lifetime income than their high school counterparts and this should be sufficient reason for you to consider going to college to sharpen your educational skills and land into a successful, worthwhile career.

Once you are in college, you need to concentrate on more than the acquisition of a college degree. You need to develop other skills, too. Like communication and leadership skills. Like organizational ability, public speaking skills and proficiency in many different facets. Participation in co-curricular activities is a must as this teaches you to relate to others in a positive manner; it also assists you in working cooperatively with others towards fulfillment of a common result.

Time management skills are crucial to your success in College and in your career. Enrolling in a time management seminar is important as a way of developing your ability to do a lot of work in little time. Speed-reading is valuable in helping you manage your time, too. In addition, general reading on diverse subjects should give you a panoramic view of the World ahead and the options available to you.

The most important advice I can give you is to focus on two things, firstly focus on what you really like doing, which is synonymous with the areas of interest you have. Secondly, make a commitment to psychological testing to determine where your strengths and weaknesses are ----- this will help you zero in on the right career path. In this matter, taking the assistance of your Vocational Assessment and Counseling unit in your school or college will assist tremendously.

In addition, Summer Internships and other summer assignments will create a strong sense of discipline and help you understand what your work responsibilities could be in the future in terms of dealing with people and completing assigned tasks perfectly within the time permitted. You will also inculcate a sense of accountability to your clients, a value not to be scoffed at. Summer work would also be a neat way for you to meet other like-minded individuals and network, which would help you forge good friendships and assist in the achievement of your future dreams. Henry Ford said something which went like this, "The only two things which create security are the people you know (networking) and the skills you have." How true this saying is. There is no guaranteed security plan in a job or business and your greatest security comes from the knowledge and support of your networking centers and the development of your education, skills and work experience so you can adapt and modify your work to any field you enjoy (working in).

Now where does positive thinking come into this academic equation? For one thing, academic study involves a long period of sacrifice and it is sometimes a challenge for a young mind to accept and implement the discipline required to work hard in school and college. A positive thinking attitude will assist greatly in terms of setting your goals lucidly and help you stay motivated, enthusiastic and brimming with energy when times are tough. Positive thinking will avoid depression and frustration and create a wellspring of energy, which can be used for the fulfillment of your goals.

Another thing I truly believe with respect to college study is the concept of "time capsulation". What this means, in simple language, is setting out your whole week's agenda in writing, a week before. A study plan will happen by focusing on one subject for a predetermined period of time (time capsulation). Once you set your time blocks, then the challenge remains to follow it as closely as you can. At the end of the week, log your actual results and compare these to what you originally set out to do.

When you look at these two pictures ask yourself the question: Where did I do well? Where did I not do that great? What lessons can I learn from this week's application (of my time energy)? And if I were to have this week to do again, what would I do differently?

One approach with which I had great success in college was to study only from Monday 10 a.m. to Friday 6 p.m. After Friday, 6 p.m., I would throw my books away till the following Monday. The weekend was reserved for rest and relaxation. I found this weekend rest assisted me in coming back to my study with a very fresh mind. This approach, among other things helped me in topping my MBA class with straight A's. It is an approach you should try.

Another suggestion I have, but something, which may prove difficult for most of you, is the philosophy and principle that no "girl/boy dating" is permitted Monday to Friday of every week when you study. You need to be focused completely on your work for maximum success. Dating girl's/boy's mid-week becomes a very distracting process and definitely takes away from your study efficiency.

In terms of your actual study process, I would recommend you study in solid blocks of time. That is, you allocate, say, a two hour block of time to study a specific subject. And after that, you rest for an hour and then you start again. Try to determine what your maximum time capacity for study per day is. Some people max out at 6 hours of study, others can go 8-10 hours per day. Try to find out the maximum period of time you can study daily without getting very tired. That time period becomes your saturation point for the day. The key to success in academic study in college is not how many hours you can study daily but how effectively you can retain all the material. Therefore a 6 hour study pattern could outperform an 8 or 9 hour study day if the student feels enthused while studying for 6 hours, has a positive minded approach to learning new things and also rests in between sessions, thus believing that he is using all his skills, interests and energy in absorbing the material effectively. And this is further confirmed by his validation of mental capacity, which justifies his capacity to study for that optimum period of time without losing retention of the material.

Positive thinking is crucial to academic success. Try to associate with other people who are positive minded or at the least, not negative in their approach to study. You just cannot afford to make friends who drag you down emotionally and intellectually. Creating a small group of highly motivated individuals in a similar class or program will help in creating a common energy bond, which will assist in the timely understanding of class work-----this approach helps you keep the positive spirit alive as you strive to excel in your Studies.

CHAPTER 7

POSITIVE THINKING AND MEDITATION/YOGA AS STRESS BUSTERS

The life of a teenage student is a fast and challenging one. And with the natural physical energies endowed in this young person, there are always numerous outlets for his time and energy. His boundless physical energy allows him to quickly adapt to his environment. However during this adaptation, some stress and pressure is bound to rise to the surface. Tensions surface when marks in class are not up to par, or if there are disciplinary issues or if the teenage student shows very little interest in his subject matter.

At times of stress and frustration, nothing beats the application of Yoga and Meditation as natural stress busters. First let us talk about Yoga. The concept of Yoga originated in India and has deep significance for East Indians, including a very spiritual value. However, in developed countries like the US, Europe and Canada, only the physical aspect of Yoga is known, understood and practiced.

One of the basic forms of Physical Yoga is called Hatha Yoga, a series of postures and exercises, including breathing techniques which help relax a person. And so, with a teenager, that may be a good point to start with. A typical Hatha yoga class lasts around 30-40 minutes and is a good mental and emotional workout for a teenager. I would encourage every teenager to find the nearest Yoga studio to his home and spend some time there to determine if this is the right thing for him. Most Universities also offer Yoga classes at very reasonable prices.

Meditation on the other hand is a deeper spiritual process, one, which many students in the Western world are not ready to undertake. As a teenager, I would regularly meditate for an hour to two every day and this practice helped me develop a sense of calmness and positivism, which helped me become more aware of my feelings and my relationships with others. I will encourage all teenagers to undertake a basic meditation program with a view to improving their performance in school and as a way of accentuating their power of awareness. The more you understand yourself in relation to others, the more you can grow as a person-----this in turn will assist you in communicating more effectively with young and old alike.

I would start by suggesting a very simple meditation exercise. I would recommend a teenage does this twice a day, once on waking up and once before sleeping. The reason I suggest you do it twice, is because in the morning, the mind has just started its conscious thinking and any affirmations, prayers and positive strokes you give yourself, the better your day will go. In the nighttime, before you sleep, a little meditation will allow your mind to reconstitute itself during sleep so you do not get troubled by any aspects or issues you experienced in the preceding day.

For the daytime, I would suggest you sit erect in a quiet place in your house. Keep your spine erect and close your eyes. Stop all your usual distractions like TV, Internet, Cell phone, and etcetera. When you are quiet and undisturbed by your external environment, start watching thoughts flood your mind. Do not engage in any particular thought; merely watch them as an observer. In the beginning this will be a difficult process, but with time you will improve your ability to stay quiet. The longer you can stay quiet, the better your day will go.

With respect to night meditation, one should again sit alone in a place you are comfortable with. Maintain erectness of the spine. In this session, make a mental note of everything you did in the day. Ask yourself what you did right and not that right and how can you improve what you did. This way, the mind has brought to the surface all the issues facing the day, so when you sleep, you sleep naturally and peacefully, having mentally resolved all your outstanding issues. It also helps to add prayer and affirmations to your meditation.

With respect to affirmations, you could pray to the good Lord for his grace, support and benevolence as you work hard to excel in Study. You could also add affirmations to the prayer, which assist you in becoming the best person you can be. So daytime meditation, nighttime meditation, daytime prayer and affirmation, nighttime prayer and affirmation all assist in silencing your Mind when you sleep, thereby allowing you a good and restful night's sleep.

How does positive thinking assist in the application of Meditation and Yoga?

Positive thinking, when combined with Faith increase and accelerate the beneficial effects of Yoga and Meditation. Positive thinking, in this context, means that you visualize in advance, the benefits of your time involvement with Meditation and Yoga. You visualize you are a calmer, more loving and effective human being. When you combine, Positive Thinking, Faith, Visualization with your practice of Meditation and Yoga, you compound the success of your practice. And this translates to a happier, simpler and stress-free person, who goes about his business effortlessly with Maximum Success.

Therefore, one must always complement the Power of Positive Thinking in respect to your practice of Yoga and Meditation.

CHAPTER 8

POSITIVE THINKING & STRESS MANAGEMENT

Stress is a common complaint among teenagers. However, this is not widely recognized by their parents and teachers or their peer group. Teenage stress experiences itself in the form of migraines, anger, frustration, headaches and a variety of other manifestations.

Let us first try to understand what Stress is and then we can understand it in the context of teenage issues. Stress exists in the presence of Danger, whether real or assumed. A stressor, which is a trigger in the external environment or inner thinking of Man, generates a danger signal at which point of time, there is a human reaction to such perceived Danger. If we go back to our history and look at prehistoric days, the hunter Man of a thousand years back, when confronted with a tiger, would have one or two choices: either "flee or fight". Our body responds with this reaction in modern day, too. The only difference is that in the past years, there was a real danger, like a Tiger (Stressor), ready to gobble you up, which caused this reaction. In today's time, the Danger can express itself in the form of a Stressor, which is Real or Unreal (Imagined). What could cause an unreal danger to express itself? A good example is Anxiety causing a "Fight or Flee" Response. A person imagines a situation may affect him adversely. The stressor here is the Thought Image in the person's Mind, which causes him to imagine an event being real (although it is not still real, it is only in his Mind and not really expressed as Real Danger). This Unreal Mental Response to an internal psychological Stressor has got this person uptight----- he is now in a "fight-flee" response physically. However, there is no place for him to run. He is still in his own physical environment. So what does such a person do? He fortifies his anxiety and tries to fight the fear mentally, but this makes his condition worse. The "fight-flee" reaction then causes psychosomatic stress, which is a condition where the reaction to the stress appears to manifest itself physically in the body, through various symptoms like nausea, stomach ache, stomach acid burns, and in extreme conditions, even an anxiety induced heart attack.

Why am I illustrating this example of Stress? Because the same symptoms of Stress manifest themselves in Teenagers----- the expressions of that stress differ somewhat from Adults. Teenagers appear to experience as having less options to counter their stress symptoms, since they are much younger and financially/emotionally/mentally dependent on their parents for support.

Now let us look at the mind of a teenager. He is growing up and at various stages of his Life is confused in his adjustment to his environment. His parents teach him one way of Life, consciously or subconsciously------ his peer group have another set of values, which may be conflicting.

He takes his knowledge and acquired value system and interacts with his world and now there are a third set of results. At this point frustration sets in------ who is he to believe in? And how is he to muster the Courage to live a life with beauty, passion and enjoyment? How is he to gain a newfound knowledge and power to live Life on his own terms? And does he really know what he wants? Does he really care to know? Or is he moving along with his peer group in the same directionless Life?

The first challenge to positively overcome this stress dilemma is to give the teenager the power to understand his predicament. And this power must necessarily come from a firsthand knowledge of what Stress is and how it affects him. The teenager must be able to clearly see the causes of his Stress, the Stressors in the environment triggering this Reaction and also be cognizant of the manifestations of this Stress, be it in the form of him suddenly being quite and withdrawn or at other times being very rebellious at home or in a state of headache, pain or other physical manifestation. At this stage of Life, it is the Parent's responsibility to be aware of his youth child's affliction. The Parent needs to be both an educator and motivator at this stage; the parent needs to educate the teenager on the causes and manifestations of Stress, on an understanding of the various Stressors causing this condition and guide him out of the jungle of pain and frustration.

Teenagers would be well advised to read a few books on Stress Management and attend a few classes, including viewing lectures on this subject, whether these lectures are presented on U-Tube or any other electronic medium or in the form of a CD or Mp3 presentation available at any good library.

The key concern here is that lack of an understanding of Stress and its negative effects could lead to brilliant, well intentioned teenagers not being able to focus appropriately on their study and co-curricular activity and thus create a life of failed grades and possibly a drop out from School. And nothing could be worse than this outcome for a teenager. I have seen and heard of numerous teenagers in North America getting into the habit of drinking, loafing around and wandering aimlessly with a like bunch of wasters. This indeed is a Life poorly wasted on wine, woman and song.

Positive thinking is a life saver, because it attacks the stress issue indirectly. A positive attitude to Life, a faith that one can change one's condition, a belief that one has the ability to change one's Life circumstance can help this teenager move out of this jungle of stress and pain and try to give him a Real chance at succeeding in Life. The more books a teenager reads on Positive Thinking, the more positive thinkers he associates it, the better his associations with chosen role models, the greater the chance of Teenage Success.

If you are a teenager and are reading this page, I would encourage you to stay positive at all times. To create a yearning for better conditions, to work hard in the presence of economic and psychological adversity at home, to reject any parental negative influence will all help you excel.

And above all, using the Power of Attraction to change your Life will make you a better, happier and more successful Student and Life Leader- a beacon of hope to other Teenagers.

CHAPTER 9

POSITIVE THINKING AND PEER PRESSURE

Peer pressure is a real and present danger for most teenage students. Let me first explain what I mean by the phrase, "Peer pressure." A peer may be considered a reference point for a teenager. This peer may represent a group of other teenagers, who he looks for guidance, support and encouragement and value assimilation as he goes on with his Life. In numerous times during a day, this teenager is either in School or in the company of his friends. In North America, Life has become so disjointed family wise, which the teenager gets to spend less and less time with his parents and more and more time with his school friends. So with this over-concentration of energy reliance on his back up system of friends, the teenager ultimately reflects the value of such chosen group of friends.

Peer pressure can therefore be very positive or extremely negative. We are now measuring a positive or negative effect in terms of its effect on the chosen Life of the teenager as he grows and expresses himself.

The challenge with peer pressure is that in many instances the teenager has very little choice in the process of choosing his peer group. The teenager is born in a certain area of the country. If he grows up in an inner city area, then he is exposed to lower level, negative energy sources with very little aspiration to improve their lot. This is in contrast to teenagers growing up in a rich neighborhood. This assumption does not always hold good, though. Inner city kids have been known to excel in their Studies and Life and richer teenagers have been shown to waste their life in spite of all the opportunities afforded to them. However, the point I am trying to make is that a teenager living in challenging conditions at home or in the geographical area of his school and friends, has a greater task of improving his attitude and Life result.

And how is one to transform this young teenager into a Life Success, particularly when the flavor of the month is a new video game or a crazy TV show? How does he become a different yet unique person who is willing to make the necessary changes to live a more fulfilling Life? The transformation is a challenge in most instances but is possible. That is one of the reasons for this book---- to produce a beginning path for all teenagers, whether Life challenged or not to find a worthwhile way to reach their dreams.

The Law of Attraction prophesizes that everything and anything is possible. The real challenge, though, is making the Teenager believe in his dream as he sees a lot of negative results in his environment and the world beyond. People being mugged; people being shot at and disastrous negative news are on television everyday-------how does such teenager disassociate himself from all this negativism? One simple way is to turn off the news and television.

Another way is to waste less time on video games and senseless internet surfing. But the motivation for this is hard to find in most teenagers. There exists the need for more guidance for teenagers to improve and expand their Life. And this motivation must firstly come from their near and dearest ones---- their Parents.

How does Positive Thinking relate to the negative effects of peer pressure? It is firstly with acceptance by the teenager that positive thinking is the fastest way for him to get from point A(where he is at now) to point B, the destination of his dreams. In terms of its connection with peer pressure, an awareness on the teenager's part that some of the values, thoughts and actions of his peer group may indeed be damaging to his future, will then result in his conscious attempt to disassociate himself from his peer group and just choose a handful of friends, who are positive and helpful------this will now start a new and modified journey towards a more meaningful Life.

Better to have a few good friends than a lot of rotten ones. When peer pressure causes a teenager to act in a certain way to please his friends, then the awareness that one needs to go on one's own chosen path and not be swayed is most important.

In India, there is a story, which was often repeated to me as a child. There is the story of a flowering plant called the "Kamal," which is the Indian translation of a lotus plant. I do not know if you have seen a lotus, but it is a very beautiful plant, which only grows in marshland. In the presence of all the muck, odor and lack of oxygen in marshland, this typical plant forms a circle of leaf to envelop the water and suddenly from nowhere sprouts a flower in the center of this circle----the flower miraculously and providentially grows in a straight line upwards, ever reaching the sky. The moral of the story is that you need to accept that there is positive and negative energy in this world and that you have a choice in a very negative environment to reach out to the sky like a lotus plant and come out different and positive. You are aware of the environment but choose to lead a different Life filled with grandeur and beauty. And such is possible in any teenage environment in any part of the World.

Positive thinking at all times, accompanied with a trust that the Universe will take care of you and your needs, with a firm determination and desire to express your dream, will get a teenager flying high in the sky. It is really possible to be anything you wish to be---to reach the Stars, if you truly want to.

CHAPTER 10

POSITIVE THINKING AND THE ROLE OF PUBLIC SPEAKING

Public Speaking can play a major role in Teenage Success. What, in fact, is Public Speaking? Public Speaking is a process of developing the confidence to express clearly your thoughts and ideas in front of large groups of people. Public Speaking is an Art form, which can be learnt through understanding and implementation of the basic principles of Public Speech. Through practice and rehearsal, one can effectively elevate one's stature in interpersonal communication.

Why is it important for a teenager to consider learning how to speak in public? These are some of the good reasons:

1. To raise your level of self-confidence.
2. To improve your level of self-esteem.
3. To become a better communicator.
4. To be able to express clearly what you want and to enable you to get what you wish.
5. To stand up for your rights and not allow anyone to run over you or exploit you.
6. To help you become a leader in every situation.
7. To help you impress people of your point of view.
8. To be able to acquire new friends through your power of speech.
9. To be able to achieve your personal, college and career goals by expressing yourself lucidly, with no fear.

I would like to relate my experiences in Public Speaking as a teenager. When I was in School, I was a successful debater and took part in many Inter-Class Debating Competitions. However, I literally froze, when called to speak in front of a very large group of people (during a Social event). I became very nervous and self-conscious. I started stuttering and my speech was impaired. I simply could not get my point across due to my intense nervousness. I had always assumed that if I could debate well, then public speaking would be a breeze. But it did not turn out that way. I was, in fact, quite disturbed by this erroneous assumption on my part. So I enquired about joining a professional Public Speaking program, which was being sponsored by the Indo-American Society in Mumbai, India. I spent a good six months learning how to craft my speech; I learnt to assemble speech material mentally in short spans of time so as to enable me to present a talk extemporaneously (with very little advance preparation) I found that at the end of the six month program, I was not only the winner of the Class Public Speaking Trophy but more importantly, had overcome my fear of talking to large groups of people.

This extra confidence carried through in my early, mid and latter years of work as I strived and attained positions of Leadership and Strength.

For a teenager, Public Speaking will give you the ability to think quickly and to express your ideas lucidly, with no fear whatsoever. It will also give you the opportunity to stand up to bullies in both the classroom and your peer group and give you strong reasons to defend yourself. Most important, it will elevate you to position of leadership in and out of the class, thereby elevating your respect among other teenagers. It will also give you the opportunity to attract some real nice friends, who are impressed by your ability to think and act clearly.

What is the role of positive thinking in public speech? Positive thinking helps you to eliminate the fear experienced by new public speakers. A positive attitude will allow you to experiment with numerous techniques used by successful speakers. It will also allow you to visualize that one day you can reach that level of grandeur and professionalism associated with master public speakers.

A word of advice. Do not necessarily feel dejected if you cannot attend and complete a professional Public Speaking Program. There are numerous wonderful books on the subject of Public Speaking available in the library or which can be ordered online. Another brilliant idea for teenagers is to join a prestigious group called Toastmasters. They are situated in every major city in North America. This group grooms young and old alike in the art of Public Speaking and gives you an opportunity to speak in front of groups regularly, thereby enhancing your skills and confidence.

Public Speaking is a vital part of the growth and development of a teenager----it provides all participants with the necessary skills, confidence and experience to put a point across and convince people of this cause. Do make regular Public Speaking a part of your co-curricular activity. Believe me; it will do wonders for you and your future.

CHAPTER 11

POSITIVE THINKING & DEALING WITH CHANGE

Change is a given in a young teenager's Life. As the young person grows to adulthood, he goes through various psychological stages. First, you start as an adolescent trying to find your way in the World with new friends----this then translates into new experiences, finally culminating in an experience with your first date in high school. As you grow and develop more relationships, there are new challenges ahead like having to excel in Study and coping with volatile family situations. It is without a question a known fact that you as a teenager are constantly bombarded with change. And how you change and adjust in your Life, determine to a great deal what you become and achieve later on. If change is accepted wholeheartedly and with a spirit of willingness, then adjustment comes easily. If there is a strong resistance to change, then the impact of such resistance is great on your young mind.

So, as a teenager, how is one to face change? This is unfortunately a subject, which is never taught in School and College. It is assumed that one has the wherewithal to make all adjustments to change, whether one is good or inept in it. Why it is that no one discusses Stress Management in School or College? Or why there is not an entire subject devoted to Human Relations and Change in Class? How is a young teenager to understand, adapt and excel in intense periods of change in his Life? Society, Parents and Peer Groups expect a teenager to follow their lead. So a teenager lands up doing what his parents may have done to adjust to a certain change or what his friends feel and act in terms of responding to Change. Very infrequently, does the teenager independently determine the cause of Change in his environment, or ponder what would be the right course of action to adapt successfully to this Change.

So, parents need to be the front line of defense here. They need to educate their children wisely of the fact that Change is inevitable---- parents have to become catalysts in making the young teenager discover fun and a challenging experience in the process of adapting to new people and new situations. A lot depends on the attitude of the teenager. A teenager has two choices ahead of him: either he can adapt easily to change with no resistance and be more effective or he forces himself to adapt with great resistance to change, which causes ultimate failure in his perceived action.

Ultimately, it appears that you, the teenager in North America have only yourself to count on to understand Change, to be aware of what is happening in your environment------- you need to muster the courage and strength to face change effectively.

A normal reaction of a teenager to change is one of initial suspicion and/or trepidation. There is fear lurking in the background in terms of how he should adapt to something new in his Life. Change is then viewed as being destabilizing and threatening to his routine. Since the net result of Change cannot be clearly seen at the present moment, there is an additional fear of lack of security since the teenager does not know the final result of the Change, which will only express itself sometime in the future. Therefore an open attitude combined with maximal awareness and an honest spirit of enquiry will go a long way in helping a teenager understand Change.

A positive attitude that Change has arrived in his life to provide a new experience, which will be beneficial long-term, will make the acceptance of change that much easy for him. Positive attitude accompanied with the power of attraction philosophy that a Change will create an impetus for the teenager to learn new things (followed by the use of this knowledge to attract the things he wants in his Life) creates a new path for such teenager. With the right approach, the right positive attitude and employment of the Law of Attraction, this teenager can climb mountains. To him now, every change is welcome, because he knows he will grow with that experience. He is now in a non-resistant state and therefore more open to adapting successfully to the change.

Positive thinking is the elixir, the magic substance, which makes Change meaningful and welcome to a teenage world. Accept Change and your Life will change for the better. Fight change and you will become weak, depressed and ineffective in your dealings with others. Which road would you choose---- a Life of positivism and happy acceptance of change or one of resistance to change accompanied with loneliness and depression????

CHAPTER 12

POSITIVE THINKING AND PUBERTY

Puberty is a particularly challenging time for teenagers. For as the hormones change, there is an indication of the readiness of the physical organism to enter the period called adulthood. Particularly in females, there are many signs of puberty manifested: more changes in emotional behavior, the development of the mammary glands and other factors showing the girl is now turning into a young woman. Such changes are also evident in males. Males show signs of change in voice intonation and increased depth of vocal chords transforming their talk from that of a grown child to one of an adult entering into a new physical state. Emotional changes are also evident.

As life's cycle changes with the onset of puberty, numerous psychological challenges come to the forefront. Particularly noteworthy is the fact that the adjustment to change is not only happening at a physical level but also at a deeper emotional level. The reaction to change becomes an irrational, emotional reaction as the young teenager tries hard to adapt to his environment, If not properly assisted by his parents, he is prone to adopting dangerous behavior like smoking cigarettes secretly, getting actively involved in dating girls with an extraordinary curiosity and engagement in sexual behavior. These tendencies are seen in the teenage population right across North America.

Parents need to be particularly sensitive to their children at this growth stage— alas; most North American parents are so occupied with their own personal lives and the numerous issues surrounding them that they merely give lip service to assisting their teenage children. And so, the teenager is left to fend for himself, psychologically. This is the stage of life, when he is most vulnerable to bad influence of his peer group---- this is also a dangerous time for the teenager because chances of accepting poor values and engaging in illegal and poor behavior increases.

And so, as usual, we come to the fact that most teenagers need to grow up on their own. Such a teenager has two choices in front of him: either reflect a negative behavior (matching the attitude of his friends and peer group) or to develop positive values on his own. But being young and afflicted with puberty related issues, how is the teenager to muster the courage to strike out on his own? On one hand, he has no independent source of income while on the other hand so many people are telling him what he is expected to do. His financial dependence may affect his independence in thought.

Unfortunately, there is no easy solution to this period called "puberty". Teenagers need to be aware of their changed emotional and physical state; they need to accept the onset of emotions, which often are irrational, they need to see the vulnerability in their systems during this critical phase of their Life.

Positive thinking can have a great impact on the teenager in this phase of Life. Positive thinking infuses a hope in teenagers that this puberty phase will also go away in due course and that Life can continue to be more organized and rational as their bodies and hearts adjust to this massive change in them----- change which creates great pain as they transform their life from a position of childhood to adulthood.

Understanding the causes and effects of puberty by reading on the subject, consulting with other positive thinking books for teenagers can also assist greatly. There has now sprung up an entire collection of books specially geared for teenagers in North America; this shows the importance of teenagers in our Society and their future value to civilization. The internet should also be accessed to view articles, viewpoints and stories on how teenagers have overcome the problems surrounding puberty.

The Law of Attraction is a very useful learning companion in this process. If the teenager is taught to write down his goals, if he is allowed to flourish in a positive spirit and taught to believe he can achieve whatever he chooses to focus his mind on, if he is encouraged to think big and experiment with new ideas and techniques, then such teenager instead of focusing on the negative physical and emotional aspects of puberty will instead redirect his focus and Energy on his goals and plans for the future. With a clear picture of who he is and where he wants to go, his journey and transformation out of puberty will be that much easier.

So, positive thinking accompanied with enthusiasm and a determination to feel well and stay well all the time, inculcation of the spirit of persistence which says that the teenager will never give up, however difficult Life may become for him and application of the Law of attraction will make a sea change in the way this teenager faces Life in Puberty and beyond.

Teenagers have the right to freedom and expression and must focus on long-term goals to help them live a more happy, stress-free and fulfilled Life. And this opportunity and freedom is available to every teenager. Are you going to claim your right to be free mentally, emotionally and spiritually or are you going to be subtly controlled by negative forces in your environment? Are you going to be the lowest common denominator of your environment or the rising star of your firmament? The choice is yours.

I truly hope you choose to be different and express yourself in your unique shape and form. And above all, that you dream big and never give up hope. Never allowing someone to tell you what you are worth and persistently progressing in the direction of your dreams will make you a successful, happy and valuable person on Mother Earth, something you should be proud of.

CHAPTER 13

POSITIVE THINKING AND LOVE

Love is the greatest quality humans are blessed with. And Love is the reason to live. Love binds people together and creates a firm foundation in human relationship. The Bible notably affirms the power of loving your neighbor and doing unto others as you would have done unto you. Love is the fresh perfume which lights the world up and gives a human a reason to Live. And in the long run, Love is the only way nations and people can come together in a spirit of joy and peace. Without Love, there is no future for Mankind as Men devise more and more cunning weapons to destroy each other.

Love is such a difficult concept for a teenager to grasp. From morning to night, this teenager is bombarded with messages across television, internet, songs and common folklore, which circumscribes love to be a unique, exclusive relationship between two people--- a Man and a Woman. The message shows two people loving each other, and then fighting with each other, then breaking up, and then reestablishing love with another, then fighting, and then breaking up, and then restarting with someone else. The love songs particularly seem to indicate not only the excitement and pleasure of physical and emotional love, but the intense pain when a couple separates. Nowhere in these messages is the important truth that Love is universal and not personal. That a mature person can Love equally his Parent, his siblings, his significant other and other living creatures and the Universe itself. Instead there are patterns of compartmentalization which compare "my love versus your love", "my happiness versus your happiness", and "my friends versus your friends". So the teenager grows up in this very polarized mental and emotional environment.

Making a change in attitude or understanding towards Love becomes very difficult for such teenager. So how does this teenager learn to look at things differently? By noticing that there is something fundamentally wrong with the way people love each other. He has to look at the results all around him. All these adults who profess they have the last word on love really live such miserable lives. It may be even in his family unit, where he lives with a single parent, where there is no love or respect between his parents or the outstanding result in North America where there is a 50 per cent failure rate in marriage. Trying to create sanity out of disorder, an honest investigation into whether there is a better way to live than to be predominantly focused on a one-to-one relationship, is the motivating factor which allows a teenager to step beyond his normal thought and relationship boundaries.

If the teenager is first taught to value friendship and see a difference between that and the definition of Love he is bombarded with; if he is taught to be patient and kind to all Living creatures around him, if he is taught to be more aware of his emotions and intellect then this would be a starting point for a modification of his Thoughts and Feelings toward the subject of Love.

If the teenager is allowed the opportunity to travel and learn about other cultures, if he is allowed to analyze what Love could signify to him, without the threat of criticism then there is a chance for a different kind of Adult to spring from this environment.

The teenager needs to understand that he is very unique and his challenge is to overcome his environment, not merely be a puppet of it. In the process he can pick and choose the positive aspects of his environment and then incorporate his own way of living based on what he has learnt and felt on his own.

Positive thinking allows this young teenager to breathe. Positive thinking gives him a hope for a better tomorrow. Positive thinking allows him the courage to experiment and analyze on his own. Positive thinking helps him stay up when he feels down.

Love is everything else than what we think it is. It starts with a reverence of Life itself. It allows you to be kind to everyone around you, including all living creatures. It gives you the permission to allow yourself the gift of staying "high" at all times. And most important it teaches you to Love yourself first, for if you cannot love yourself as you are, your faults and strengths included, you lack the capacity to love anyone else.

Love is the elixir which can create a new breed of people all bound by the same faith and principles. People living together, working together and creating a better world for themselves and their progeny. And most important, Love is a gateway to your divine connection. If you can see love in yourself and connect with that love through someone else, without wanting something in return, then that is true Love. You can acquire what you need to live but you do not do this by destroying someone else's opportunity. As the Bible exhorts, do not lie, do not cheat and do not sin. If only more people read and applied the great teachings of the Bible, the world would be a better place for all.

CHAPTER 14

POSITIVE THINKING AND MONEY SAVING HABITS

Life is an intense financial Challenge. Ever since a child grows up and learns to walk, he is bombarded with concepts, ideas and behavior surrounding the application of money. The teenager sees his parents go to work for eight to ten hours per day and come home tired. He sees the need for his parents to earn income to sustain the family unit. On several occasions, he is witness to arguments in his home----- these arguments center on opposing parental views surrounding the use of money. One parent may have bought something, without consulting the other and there is obviously a difference of opinion on perceived waste of money. As he grows up and goes to school, he is cognizant of rich and poor students. He notices how the rich students seem to be blessed with all the good things in Life and the poor and middle class struggle to make ends meet.

What happens inside his family unit has a great bearing on the teenager's attitude and value towards money. But does this teenager see the long term-picture of money? Does he understand what money is? Does he see what he must do to escape this cycle of work and pain? Does he notice how working people around him struggle and work so hard in exchange for a mere pittance? In most cases, there is no "big picture understanding" of what money is and how it could affect him for the rest of his Life.

So what is such teenager to do to get a healthy approach towards Money? Firstly, he must accept he is bound by the rules of Money. That Society has made a rule that one must work to earn money and once that money is earned it can be spent for a person's survival. This is one of the fundamental rules of money. The teenager understands and accepts that he needs to work as he grows up to meet with his personal needs, since his parents will only support him up to a point in his Life. But most important the teenager must search for a way to break this vicious cycle of work and money earned as a result of such work. By a vicious cycle, I mean a situation where more than 95 per cent of the adult population, age 18-65, are bound by golden handcuffs------they experience an economic situation where they never earn enough to meet with all their needs and desires which causes them to become puppets of their employers----in essence they sell their soul for a living. This might appear to be an over-dramatization but it is a fundamental truth of North American life. A family may enjoy a good living, which involves owning a nice home and car but their very security is totally income-centric, in the sense that a loss of income due to illness, unemployment or poor health creates devastating consequences for the family. And there is no easy solution to being financially free.

There is nothing wrong with engaging in a job you enjoy; the problem is that you never ever create financial freedom by merely working------you need something else to guarantee your Lifestyle.

Years back in sales school, I was taught there are only two ways to make money; one is to work till you almost die and earn and spend income ad infinitum ---- the other smarter solution was to have money work for you. In short, you can either work for money or you can have money work for you. Which one would you prefer? Working ceaselessly and endlessly for a little income every month all of which evaporates at the end of the month or being able to create a nest-egg, which will take care of all your needs in the future without constant work, pressure and financial anxiety. You then have the choice to work or not work, you have the choice to relax and travel and you have the opportunity to truly enjoy your Life. Most unfortunately, these concepts are not taught in school or college. This result in most people working and spending whatever they earn with no savings left to enjoy the good things in Life.

This brings me to the concept of a Savings habit. How does one accumulate a nest-egg, which can serve your needs forever? There are quick and risky methods to build such nest-egg or a solid and risk free method of doing this.

The riskier method, which is also feasible for some, is to accumulate capital through creating a business and generating value through it. It is riskier since you put your time, energy and little capital available at risk, hoping your business becomes successful.

The easier way to build the savings habit is through a systematic investment plan. I would like to point out to the ambitious teenager willing to live Life on his terms, that it is not how much money you save every month which is important as much as the fact that you do it consistently every month. And critically, once you save that money, you promise never to touch it, till it grows to a reasonable size and then only to invest in a valuable idea like owning your own home or another worthwhile financial investment project. Money has a Life of its own and if you do not touch it and allow it to grow, you will be surprised that from a tiny savings acorn you will create a massive oak tree, which will feed you for years and years into the future.

The teenager may ask how one should start the process. I would say pick a goal, say 20 per cent of everything that passes through your hands. So if you get pocket money of $50 per week, take $10 and save it. Put it in a piggy bank, or open a savings account in a neighborhood bank. The key is that once you start this process, you never ever touch this money. This money will form the foundation for you to build a nest egg for the future, so that you will reach a point of time in your future Life at say, 45 or 50 years, when you can safely retire from the rat race and live Life on your own terms.

On the other hand if you want to retire when you are 30 or 35 years and have the entrepreneurial ambition, guts and energy to take risks, then try to open up a business of your Lots of successful young people have taken a regular job and started a part time business on the side.

Life is full of endless possibilities but the savings habit is the only way to create your own fortune and allow yourself the freedom to enjoy Life to the fullest.

Positive thinking allows a teenager to visualize his future dream of owning a successful business and/or retiring early and enjoying Life to the fullest. Positive thinking gives you the courage to start your savings habit and keep the good habit up so that you give yourself enough time to build your fortune.

I hope and pray that every teenager heeds my advice and starts saving a little bit of money every month on a religious basis. You have a right to be rich, free and independent and I believe that positive thinking will help you get there faster and easier.

CHAPTER 15

POSITIVE THINKING AND COMPETITION

As more and more of us live in freer democratic societies, we get to understand that competition is in the Nature of Political and Economic Life. As the teenager grows, he learns to compete with his siblings for his parent's time and attention; as he grows a little more he starts competing with other rivals for a woman's attention. In School, he has to compete with other classmates for good grades. As he moves up the Age Ladder, he has to compete with others for a woman of his choice and then work hard to get into a good college based on his school and college grades. Life becomes a constant source of Competitive Stress as the teenage sometimes hits the mark and often does not achieve his intended objective.

So competition is looked upon as favorable when the teenager gets what he wants and as debilitating and depressing when goals do not seem to be reached as he gets passed over for friends, girl-mates and challenging co-curricular assignments. In such challenging circumstances what is a teenager to make of Competition?

I learnt years back that the only competition you faced was the one with yourself. If you decided on certain goals, which was the first requirement, then you measured your success or failure by your ability to achieve these goals. Care here had to be taken between distinguishing between your individually set standards and your parental, environmental and peer group standards. Often as a teenager growing up, I was confused with all the contradictions inevitable between what I truly desired and what others expected of me.

So, a complete and dedicated focus to what you truly desire and want and a complete exclusion of other's wishes (superimposed on you sub-consciously) is the first step. Blessed is the teenager whose parents allow him to choose whatever he wants to be, even encouraging the process. But in most cases it is the subtler influence of other so called well-wishers, which influence the teenage decision and goal-setting process.

Another technique, which I learnt in childhood, was to look in the mirror every day before I went to school and look at the reflection of myself. Now I set a goal for myself and my role was to achieve what I had set out for myself. I looked at the mirror and reminded myself of this affirmation, as I watched my reflection.

A third element of competition is to love "you". Now, you may ask, what does this have to do with competition? If there is a high level of self-esteem and confidence and trust in the Universe, and a belief that the Universal Energy will in its benevolence grant you your wishes then you start loving yourself more. You start loving yourself as you are, with all your faults and strengths and this Self-Love becomes very important, because as you enter the field of competitive activity you outperform everyone simply because you believe you are great and unique and this energy reflects itself on everything you do. This is one to the manifestations of the Law of Attraction, a Law on which we will dwell at length in a later chapter.

What does Positive Thinking have to do with Competition? Pretty much everything. If you are positive and stay positive right through your day, whether this involves classroom attendance, school homework, sports activities and contacts with friends, this self-confident energy will drive in the corresponding circumstances in the outside world and you will be able to achieve everything easily. A positive attitude will make you understand that you only compete against yourself (and your goals) and if you strive to do what you wish, then results must follow and such results will always be superlative and place you in the top of your class. This does not always make logical sense, but nor does the Law of Attraction, which defies logic. It is always a case of Mind over Matter, and if you think you can, then you probably will as long as you focus on this thought and never give up your vision to be the best you can be in the field you have chosen. Never give up on your focused thoughts and goals ------- and you will always be successful in attracting what you deserve.

Positive Thinking, use of the Law of Attraction, a dogged determination to succeed and an undying Faith in your ability to get to where you want, will eliminate the stress associated with competitive activities. Focusing on your goals and realizing you essentially are only competing with yourself will help you get to where you want, in an effortless manner. And you will have great Fun getting what you want!!!!

CHAPTER 16

POSITIVE THINKING AND CREATIVE IMAGINATION

Creative imagination is the catalyst, which creates World Progress. The pioneers, who discovered electricity, the telephone and the internet created much Positive Change in the world. People were able to live a better Life (Electricity); they were able to communicate over long distances easily (phone) and they developed an unbound reference source of knowledge (internet). Technology, aided with creative imagination, changed the way Mankind lived. It also affected how we thought and communicated with each other.

Most unfortunately, Creative Imagination is not taught in the classroom or in a College. It is assumed that you have it in an unmeasured and unspecified way. It is true that some teenagers are blessed with a more fertile imagination than others. This is sparked by a great sense of curiosity, which helps them understand their World more effectively.

But is creative imagination not a God-given right? Then why do so few teenagers employ this skill? I would say this is, firstly, due to lack of knowledge of the value of this skill. So, let us now try to understand what creative imagination is. Creativity is a new way of looking at old things. A creative spark helps a teenager put two and two together in a more effective manner. It helps one see the bigger picture more easily and effectively. Also, it provides a teenager a new and untested way of doing his homework faster, to build better relationships with his friends and to excel in his school and college work.

If such value of creative imagination is accepted by the teenager, then one can move to thinking "out of the box" and experimenting with new and unique ways of doing the same things day after day, which often appear to be boring and cumbersome for the typical teenager.

Positive thinking assists the development of a fertile and creative imagination. With positive thinking, you are constantly searching for answers to the challenges in your Life. And when you extend your positive thinking to creativity, you now get both your general thinking and your creative power to work hand-in-hand to show you new ways to do old things, to get better results in less time and to win new friends and excel in whatever you do.

A creative imagination aided with Positive thinking is an unbeatable combination. Would you not like to do your homework faster? Would you not like to retain your school and college study material quicker? Would you not like to excel in Sports? So why not start right now and use your Creative Imagination to devise new ways of doing things and fun ways of rearranging your time and priorities? You will be surprised at how much faster you reach your goals by allowing the Power of Creativity into your Life.

CHAPTER 17

POSITIVE THINKING AND THE LAW OF ATTRACTION

The law of Attraction is one of the most powerful laws in this Universe. What it dictates is that you can get anything you want, so long as you want it bad enough, that you focus consistently on this thought and believe this Thought will attract its counterpart in the Physical Universe. It is a simple yet unique way of looking at things in Life. As we grow through the teenage years, we are taught to believe solely in our Power of Rationality; the entire cultural system in North America is centered on rational principles------ one of these principles says, "You will believe it after you see it." The Law of Attraction is the exact opposite of this----- it commands that "You will see it when you first believe in it."

So, how is the Teenage Mind to be re-oriented to this powerful Law? It is basically by allowing the teenage to experiment with a new way of thinking, acting and believing. Teenagers in North America are brought up in a negative energy orientation. That is, in spite of them being so blessed with everything imaginable in terms of food, clothing, shelter and future opportunities, their Life seems to be colored by many negative energy sources, prominent among which is peer group pressure. The pressure and subsequent environment reminds me of a scene from the Bible, referred to as "Sodom and Gomorrah." In this narration from the Bible, the Israelites were freed by God from the ruthless and cruel clutches of the Egyptians and having now crossed the Red Sea, first experienced a life of personal freedom. Gone were the Egyptian tax collectors and their oppressive Egyptian king. The freed Israelites settled down in the new unknown Land, trying to move on now with their new found Life and freedom. Moses, who led the Israelites from Egyptian tyranny, went up the Mount to receive further instructions from God. These instructions came in the form of the Ten Commandments. When Moses came back from his retreat in the Mount, he saw his people engage in fun and frolic, many of whom were caught up in merriment, dance and drink. They had now started worshipping a new God---- a God shaped in the form of a golden idol. They had started worshipping idols and projected these as their God and Savior.

Current day environmental conditions in North America point out to a similar "Sodom and Gomorrah" situation. Great wealth, an abundance of food and shelter and unlimited time and money to engage in numerous pursuits like videogames, internet distractions and countless television shows have created a moral and psychological lack in North American teenagers. The ambition to achieve has been drained and there is no real progress in terms of either setting or realizing any worthwhile goal.

The Law of Attraction gives you an opportunity to do the opposite. The Law of Attraction teaches that you must first believe in yourself------ you must understand that you can attract whatever you wish by following certain laws, which guide you through this process. Through an understanding of the Law of Attraction, one learns to confront the fears which come to the surface as one has to face the inevitable choice of either believing totally in you or of choosing to live a Life based on "self-limiting beliefs".

You, as a teenager need to understand and appreciate that the Law of Attraction applies to every aspect of your Life---- that is, your Emotional, Physical, Mental and Spiritual Life. And to succeed in Life, you must learn to fine tune and integrate all these areas of your Life.

The Law of Attraction also teaches the importance of having worthwhile goals. Because without goals, life becomes a rudderless process. It is like sitting in a motor boat with no rudder so even though you crank up your engine, you are not going anywhere.

Positive Thinking is an important part of the Law of Attraction. In one short sentence, Positive Thinking is meant to emphasize that "one must go in the direction of his dream, with no fear , with the full expectation and belief that you can and will attract into your Life what you wish."

The Power of Intention allows the teenager to give himself permission to bring all the positive aspects of the law of Attraction into his Life. Prayer, Meditation and Guided Visualization all assist in bringing together your Life of distinction marked with exemplary service to fulfill other people's needs.

I would encourage all teenagers to research their library and internet resources on articles, videos, mp3's and books pertaining to the "Power of Attraction". One will come upon some wonderful ideas, concepts and principles, which when applied will make your Life not only successful but meaningful to others.

The Law of Attraction has great value and significance to you. First, you must set a tangible, quantifiable goal. Then one must set a time deadline to achieve it. While you are doing this, you must write down the reasons for the goal and what rewards you visualize achieving by completing the written goal. This must be then backed with a positive attitude and an expectation that you have already received what you planned. So, if you visualize that you have already achieved your goal before you have started your journey towards it that will make goal accomplishment easier. Then you must follow this up with a plan of Action, marking your progress towards achievement of your goal. And you must be persistent in your efforts and patient to allow the fruits of your hard work to manifest itself.

The Law of Attraction really works. Try it out for size and see how your Life changes for the better with its incorporation in your work, study and social Life.

CHAPTER 18

POSITIVE THINKING & CAREER SEARCH

Today's teenager faces massive career challenges. Not only does he need to get a first class school and university education but he must identify an appropriate career path. Going to college in America has become a very expensive proposition. Colleges and universities amass hundreds of millions of dollars--- they all offer a quick fix to the long-term income and career needs of aspiring students. It is well known that college and university education is a must for a majority of student population if they want to improve their career outlook and future income possibility. However, not well known is the fact that just going to college and/or university and getting a random degree is no assurance of success in finding a job or developing a career. I recently met a law school graduate, who had spent over $200,000 overall on her entire college and law degree education------ however, she was still not sure whether she was going to get a good law job after graduation. She still had to face the burden of paying off this mammoth loan hanging over her head. The converse part of this incredible funding challenge is that several young teenagers get so terrified about the immense financial burden (they must carry) that they totally avoid going to college. Both approaches are wrong and that is the subject matter of this chapter. One needs to accept the risk and costs of university education, but one must be very selective in terms of course and degree selection, matching inherent skills/talents closely with future job opportunities.

A teenager must take great pain and spare no effort in identifying a future career path, before he starts on his path towards a college degree. What is most important is a match between the natural traits and interests of the teenager and the possible career choices available to him. Most teenagers do this in reverse; they look around to find out which jobs are available and then satisfice, i.e. they try to adjust job and career demand and imagine that this would be a right fit in terms of their own natural interests. Nothing could be more debilitating and negative for such teenager; the young student must first identify accurately his prime interests and then try to match those with available jobs/career paths. If there is no proper match between a good career and his natural skills/talents, then he must consider expressing his natural interests and skills through the establishment of a new business.

First, let us talk about skill identification. What are the inherent skills a teenager has? Is it communication skills? Is it selling skills? Is it being a proficient public speaker? Is it extraordinary ability in Science or Mathematics? Or a fondness of World History or the English language? Care must be taken by the teenager to be totally honest with him. He needs to first, without coercion or outside influence, identify what skills he naturally possesses. Once a set of three or four skill and interest areas are identified, then he needs to identify what job/career path would suit such skills/interest areas. If he possesses sales skills, which include the art of convincing others of his cause, whether it is selling newspapers or raising money for a school charity, then the career/job choices, among others could include, insurance, financial services, and real estate.

The next challenging step is to match accurately the skill/talent endowment of a teenager with career and job possibilities. I would very strongly recommend consulting with the Vocational and Career Section in a School or College. Additionally, I would recommend the completion of specialized Psychological tests, the objective of which is to identify inherent psychological strengths and weaknesses and match these with possible career areas. Additionally, it would be valuable to know of job/career possibilities in your geographical area. Job positions vary greatly depending on which part of the country you live in. This is important, unless you do not mind leaving your roots behind and travelling far from family and friends to start a new future.

In terms of a future opportunity, a teenager is well advised to focus on a long-term career opportunity and not the achievement of a short term job situation. However, when he is brand new to the workforce, he may have to initially settle for a short term job. However, his view should be necessarily long-term as he plans to get the skills to excel in his chosen career path. Some of the lucrative job/career routes are in the field of Medicine, Engineering and Business, but everyone is not necessarily interested in these fields and even if they are, getting into the right college could prove to be difficult. As a rule, one should try to get into an Ivy League school, if possible. Although the tuition and living costs are higher there, one starts off with a higher starting salary and a better and faster upward career path. Having said this, it does not follow that a student from an Ivy League School is necessarily better than one from an average College or University; it is just the impression and image of an Ivy League college, which helps the student land a job faster. Once you are in the job, your college background is forgotten and you need to perform to keep and grow your job. However, getting into an Ivy League college is massively challenging. I just read an article where the acceptance rate at an Ivy League school was 5%. 95 out of every 100 applicants were rejected!!!! Notwithstanding that, one must still try to get into the best college/university you can get into given your academic performance and access to education funding.

If you are not much into achieving high grades, then why not try getting into a college, based on outstanding sports achievement? One needs to continually try to market and reinvent oneself to get into the best college/university and then work aggressively to market yourself, job wise, to a Fortune 500 employer, for example.

Now, what is the role of Positive Thinking in your search process for appropriate skills identification, natural talent exposure and talent/career matches? Positive thinking is very critical here, since there is a complete lack of direction at the parental and school level of appropriate career choices. Like money management, no one really takes the time and trouble to assist a teenager isolate the right career path.

Positive thinking is required for the teenager to create and maintain confidence in the identification of his natural talent and skills and in the aggressive matching of talent/skill with jobs out there. A positive attitude will assist a teenager speak with school educators, school vocational departments, with parents and other sources, with a view to being accurately informed of where the good opportunities are. And if he decides to go into business for himself, meetings with small and medium sized businessman about their experiences in business, voluntary entrepreneurial assignments in say, charity-raising or other worthwhile causes will help the teenage identify if he has what it takes to be a successful businessman. In the process, the teenager will encounter a lot of negative energy(from his peer group) surrounding his search process-----positive thinking will help support and sustain him as he marches forward with confidence to find his place in the sun.

Be sure that the ultimate responsibility for finding a career/job path belongs to you. So, with extraordinary courage, positive thinking, a dogged determination to zero in on the right career and a never failing attitude, you will identify the right career field for yourself. Do not forget, it is not just the career which is important---- Life is more crucial. What I am trying to say is if you find a quick fix to this great challenge, you may land up in a job or career for your entire Lifetime, but never be happy there. This, in turn, will create massive anxiety and frustration and a feeling that you are not happy long run. For how can one be happy, unless one really loves what one does? The right job or career is synonymous with long term happiness and stability. Therefore, look at a job or career as fulfilling your long-term needs and aspirations. You will be happier, more excited and will be successful in all fronts, career, home and personal.

CHAPTER 19

POSITIVE THINKING & ENTERPRENEURIAL SUCCESS

Economic conditions today call for a "new entrepreneurial spirit" among teenagers. In the last ten years, there has been an astronomic rise in new business formation and many of these new businesses are being started by teenagers, who cannot find any worthwhile job of their choosing. In North America, there is a great fear on part of teenagers to start a new business. Some of the concerns here are lack of funding, lack of business knowledge and lack of relevant experience. However, particularly in North America, jobs are shrinking and it is not easy for a teenager to find the right job or career. If this teenager is courageous, he may find his calling in business. However, the kind of thinking and action required to succeed in business is quite different than that required in a job.

What are the foremost qualities required for business success?

First and foremost, positive thinking is the key. The teenage must understand, accept and act on the belief that there is opportunity in business. And that he could have a more successful long-term career in business than any other field of endeavor, like working for someone else. And this new business comes with an opportunity of being your own boss, being able to plan your own time and having the ability to lead others, long-term in your business.

Secondly, the attitude towards Risk needs to be examined. Risk in business involves a massive adjustment in attitude towards the twin challenges of change and uncertainty--------this quality is something not well developed in teenagers. How does a young teenager thrust himself into the danger area called, "Risk taking?" He does this by trying at, as early an age as possible, the participation in some entrepreneurial activity. Why not get involved in a newspaper selling route? Or sell products for a charity at school? Or organize a school book event? Or direct a school play? All of these activities assist a teenager try his hands in entrepreneurial activities and give him an early indication if he enjoys this kind of activity. It also provides direction if he is successful in such entrepreneurial work. If he does achieve success here, then he must continue to develop these skills as he moves towards college and university.

In addition, there is the issue of funding. For teenagers embarking on a new business, funding is very difficult to come by. Why not be creative here? Come up with a brilliant business plan and convince your parents to loan you some money. Start with a low capital intensive business and gradually build it.

I saw a television show recently, where a young fella, maybe 25 years, dreamt up an idea of cleaning cars in a green (environmentally) sensitive way. I saw this young person, full of dreams, explaining his philosophy on Television. He said that if everyone paid more attention to the environment, the world would indeed be cleaner and greener--------- and he wanted to play a role in such development. I was so thrilled to see this young boy, with limited capital, striving to find his place in the business world. And this idea was taking off in his vicinity of business operation. People were willing to pay an extra few dollars for cleaning their cars in an environmentally friendly way. This is an example of a brilliant low capital business idea, which met with outstanding success.

Another great venture, if funding becomes an issue, is to get involved in a sales profession. Selling insurance or real estate offers a low capital method of creating your own business. What are required are excellent communication skills, a good sales personality, high goal-setting attitudes and a willingness to work hard and find new clients. Numerous teenagers have found success in insurance and real estate. What you need to do is think "outside the box" and any creative endeavor (which you enjoy) should be experimented with.

Positive thinking can aid in entrepreneurial success in the following ways:

1. Positive thinking can give you the motivation to start a new business.
2. Positive thinking can give you the courage to experiment with new ideas.
3. Positive thinking can help you "stick your neck out" and look for funding sources.
4. Positive thinking can instill a courageous attitude, which never gives up and keeps allowing you to try harder and harder till you succeed in your new business.
5. Positive thinking can help you set aside all negative thinking of individuals in your peer group and/or your parents, who may discourage you from trying something new or risking your time and capital in a new untested venture.
6. Positive energy can give you a healthy outlook towards new business risk.
7. And positive thinking can help you succeed, where others have failed, ensuring a happy and successful career for yourself---- a career you have crafted through your natural talent and skills.

Remember, positive thinking + persistence + courage + enthusiasm + risk taking + clear goals = business success.

You could be the next young millionaire in North America!!!!!!!!!

CHAPTER 20

POSITIVE THINKING AND GOAL SETTING/VISUALIZATION

Everything worthwhile in Life starts and ends with a Goal. Alas, how little teenagers are taught about Goal Setting. No courses exist in their curriculum, which help them understand how to set goals, how to measure their progress towards getting what they want and how to actually achieve their goals. Like learning how to manage money, goal-setting is one of the most ignored areas of study in North America.

What is goal setting? How can we define it precisely? Very simply, goal setting is "the worthwhile realization of a predetermined goal?" Let us now go deeper into the basic definition of goal setting. What is a predetermined goal? It is a goal, which offers value to the teenager. It becomes a predetermined objective when you put it down in writing. Then, to be effective that particular written goal must be accompanied by a deadline for its accomplishment. You must know by what date you commit to achieving your goal, otherwise the goal has no meaning. Then, most importantly, ask yourself what rewards you will achieve by putting the time and energy to achieve the predetermined worthwhile goal. The rewards are very important to quantify. Now you are ready to realize your goal. Each and every step above, the writing of the goal, the deadline associated with it, the written plan of action to achieve it and the rewards which you will enjoy on fulfilling the goal are crucial in its attainment.

What is visualization? It is a process of imagining that you have already attained the goal, even before you start the work towards getting what you want. Is this a form of irrational exuberance? You bet it is. However, believe me, this attitude works in creating (goal achievement) success faster. Your mind is a powerful mechanism and whatever you believe in will manifest itself in your Life, sooner or later. The more you believe in a specific goal or outcome, the sooner you will see it manifested in your Life. This is an example of the Law of Manifestation. Visualization, when aided with positive thinking accelerates your process of achievement.

Positive thinking helps you dream big; it challenges you to set goals, which are not way beyond your capacity, but something you can see yourself stretch towards. Positive thinking also helps you stay your course when times get tough. And when accompanied with visualization, it moves you quickly in the direction of your dreams.

As we all know, nothing succeeds like Success and Positive Thinking, Visualization and goal-setting all help you get what you want in the least possible time with the least stress. This is Maximum Performance!!!!!!!

CHAPTER 21

POSITIVE THINKING AND MOTIVATION

Motivation is the greatest Living force, which propels someone from Point A to Point B. Point A is referred to as a starting point of goal achievement---- it represents the present moment of time, while Point B is a future time defined as "happening" when you achieve your goal. For a teenager, understanding and implementing the Law of Motivation is very important in realizing his Success and Happiness. However, we know so little about Motivation. The subject of Motivation is never taught in classrooms. Even adults know so little about how to use Motivation in their careers and businesses.

So where does a teenager start with this process called Self-Motivation? By understanding it is a very powerful Law. Using this Law helps him with achievement of great success------- avoidance or ignorance of the Law results in a Teenager taking very long to get to where he wants to go.

Motivation is an energy source. I like to explain it as a Life catalyst. For those of you teenagers, who have studied chemistry, you know that a catalyst is a substance, which in small quantities, induces a massive chemical reaction. In the same way, motivation is a Life catalyst. Your teenage Life consists of a lot of humdrum activity. But, add the catalyst called "Motivation", and there is an explosion. And that explosion moves you faster to achieving your dreams and goals. It is extremely difficult to quantify how Motivation does this miraculous act or to describe in great detail how Motivation impacts your Life. It is sufficient to say that it causes a beneficial and massive reaction. Simply put, it is a drawing Force, which moves you beyond mountains to that ideal place you wish to be in. However, Motivation must be guided by principles and value systems and be accompanied with goal setting, which we discussed in the last chapter.

How do you know if a teenager is motivated? How do you know he is charging like a bull in the achievement of his dreams? Watch a successful teenager in action. As they say, "you can see it in his eyes". His eyes gleam with pride, his spirit expresses an indomitable streak, his chin and face show a deep resolve and his face lights up every time you discuss his pet project. We have all seen these physical traits in other successful people, but do we try to adopt these traits in ourselves? And do we investigate what it is that drives these people to remarkable levels of success? Very few of us take the time and trouble to understand what makes successful people tick.

First, one needs to identify where one is heading. Living a life without goals is like managing a boat without a rudder. If you apply the throttle to a rudderless boat, the engine revs up but you go nowhere. You just spin at a high speed in the same position and location you exist in. Therefore having a rudder (goal) in your boat is crucial to your ability to move ahead at incredible speed. The rudder guides the boat at the speed and direction you want to steer in and without this rudder, there is no hope for movement and progress. For a teenager, the earlier he starts setting goals and achieving them, the more successful he will be in later life. Starting out, set simple, easily achievable goals. The simpler, relatively easy goals you achieve, the more confidence you will develop. This will help you further in Life, when goals can become quite complex.

Along with setting realistic and worthwhile goals, one needs to go on this journey armed with a spirit of positive thinking. Because without positive thinking there can be no progress, however lofty your goals are. So what is positive thinking? It really is a state of Mind, but it is more than that. It is a way of Living a Life with hope and passion. It is living in the present, knowing that you will get everything you want and deserve. Positive thinking is closely linked to the Law of Attraction and works hand-in-hand with that. Positive thinking, enthusiasm, determination, visualization, goal setting and the Law of Attraction all form one complete circle. You will see constant reference made to these terms in this book, since these components are all intrinsically part of a whole. The more you learn to use all these components in your Life together, the more successful you will be.

What is the value of motivating yourself? This must be foremost in a young teenage mind. Naturally, the value of self-motivation is its role in helping you get what you want in the quickest amount of time with the maximum amount of Success. This understanding of your reward structure will help you realize the value of self-motivation. And every time you feel down, you use positive thinking to remind you of why you are working so hard and what you seek to gain from all this. You have to constantly focus on your rewards.

If you are a teenager and want to have your first convertible before age 19, then you have to constantly focus on the reward and then your going will become easy. Why not cut a picture of your favorite convertible and stick it everywhere------ in your room, in front of your refrigerator, on top of your workbooks and any other place you frequent. Look at this picture fifty, one hundred, five hundred times a day. The more you are reminded of your reward, the faster you will achieve it. This is the irrefutable Law of Motivation combined with the Law of Attraction.

Anything and everything is possible if you put your Mind to and focus on that thought religiously. Self-Motivation is a method of taking responsibility for your motivation process. Positive thinking helps you get maximum benefit from Self-Motivation. May it be a fountainhead to help you have a brilliant Life filled with all nice things, which make you happy and fulfilled in every Way possible!!!!

CHAPTER 22

POSITIVE THINKING & ROLE MODELING

In this world of intense competition, strife and nonstop motion, it is critical for a teenager to get a hand in achieving success by good "role modeling". A positive and successful role model serves as an inspirational source for a teenager, thereby helping him achieve his goals and dreams easily. When you look at the World at large, you see so many different individuals, institutions and advertising platforms all vying for your attention. Once advertising platforms get your attention, they try to sell you on the value of their product or service. In North America, hundreds of millions of dollars are being spent in advertising to promote a certain brand or service image; before they can promote this image, they need to get you to believe that a certain kind of lifestyle is best for you, the teenager. Once they are able to convince you of that, then they provide a product offering, like a pair of jeans as the right solution to your need to stay up there with "the Joneses". If you look at the history of jean marketing in North America, people initially started wearing jeans because it was made of cotton and was comfortable to get in and around your tasks in Life. This slowly changed to boot cut jeans, narrow jeans and tight jeans and God knows how many new marketing variations. Now you see young teenagers wanting to purchase the ultra-tight jeans because they look nice and sexy. Now, there is no harm in wearing fashionable clothes, but the point is the danger of any teenager accepting this to be the beginning and end of his Life. By this, I do not mean that ultra tight jeans are the beginning and end of your teenage universe but how advertisers try to force this perception down your throat------ and if you accept this perception then you get influenced into believing these messages, which then shape you and your actions. Are you really aware of how these advertiser sponsored values are shaping who you are? The reason I give this example, is that teenagers need to break the mould in order to be successful.

Role-modeling is the first stage of this transformation process. The teenager now looks for real examples of people in their environment, whether such environment is the news, television, radio, and internet or family friends who they feel comfortable emulating. Care must be taken by the teenager to pick role models, who express admirable qualities like honesty, hard work, talent and success. If you pick a role model who is currently aligned in your future chosen field of endeavor that would be even better. So, if you want to be a stock car driver and one day plan to race the Indy 500 as a champion, try to find a role model who is currently an outstanding championship stock car driver now.

The best role models would ideally be the ones nearest and dearest to you, but alas all parents do not make good role models. For example, if your father is an alcoholic or your mother spends all day shopping on TV, you need to ask yourself if these are appropriate role models.

So many teenagers just get influenced by their family environment and peer group that they subconsciously start reflecting the values of these people who are very close to them. They then fashion their lives based on what they see around them----- as a result, they attract failure and much unhappiness in their lives since they are modeling their behavior and values on the failures of others, however much these individuals love them.

So the first principle that must be grasped is that you need to be different to be successful. If you do what everyone else is doing, then you become the lowest common denominator of your chosen group. So, a teenager, must ask himself seriously what he wants to do with his Life---- this Life and Time belongs to him and therefore it is not only his responsibility to live well in this time provided to him by the Universal Energy, but also to pick the right situation, the right environment and the right career for himself. This process calls for a great deal of Soul Searching. It also involves coming to terms with yourself and the positive and negative influences of your environment. Why not sit by yourself in a quiet place and enumerate the dominant positive and negative values in your special environment? Then with the stroke of a pen cross out all the negatives in your environment. With the remainder positive list, add the other desirable positive factors you wish for in your current Life----- this will assist you greatly in defining and implementing successfully a long-term career or job goal. Then work towards achieving it.

Positive thinking gives you the strength to "carry your cross". It provides you with the courage to keep moving ahead in the direction of your dreams. It gives you the strength to overcome negative values in the environment and to surpass all expectations you place on yourself. Positive thinking, when engaged, on a continual basis, also gives you the power to set your own dreams and goals and arms you with the belief and knowledge that you can achieve your predetermined goals, using the Law of attraction to guide you.

Role-modeling, when assisted with the power of positive thinking, gives you the inner motivation and momentum to achieve whatever you choose to do. It allows you to get what you want faster than would otherwise be possible.

CHAPTER 23

POSITIVE THINKING &
SELF-CONCEPT/SELF-IMAGE TRANSFORMATION

The Mind is the most powerful working instrument we own. With our Mind, we experience our World and choose to brighten our experiences or attract a lot of misery and unhappiness. Teenagers, unfortunately, are taught how to think by their parents and their peer group. Their methods of thinking follow a certain mechanical routine based on values derived in their immediate environment. As they grow and express themselves in their school and personal life, they develop two parallel concepts, a self-image and a self-concept. And the collision of these concepts determines how successful a teenager is and how he expresses his Life in the future. Now let us get down to an understanding of self-concept and self-image.

Self-image is the particular image a teenager has about who he is----- in this image is embedded his ideas and opinions on how smart or dumb he is, his reflection of his physical strengths, his presumption of his ability to convince others, and his perception of how much intelligence and self-confidence he possesses. These are just a few of the values embedded in his self-image. In fact, all attributes of his personality, as known, believed and experienced by the teenager reflect his "total self-image".

Self-concept is the way the teenager perceives how others view him in his very special external world. So self-concept is a sum total of all impressions, values, opinions and understanding of a teenager's strength and weakness as perceived by his parent, his peer group and the world at large. Do note that this impression is framed by the teenager himself.

Why is it so important to understand self-image and self-concept??? Because the variation in these two images impacts the Life and Success of a teenager. And this impact is quite dramatic.

Let us look at an illustration. Let us assume that the teenager's self-image is one that he is lazy (he thinks he is lazy). However his self-concept, or the way he perceives others seeing him is as a very hard working kid. Obviously, we have a conflict here. The teenager will probably continue to be lazy since he has misunderstood how his behavior impacts others. Let us now turn the table around; let us suppose the teenager thinks he is hard working (self-image) but others view him as being lazy (self-concept). So the teenager thinks he is a hard worker, but his results are very poor in school. How does this conflict get resolved? By the teenager honestly looking at the number of hours he studies in school and how well he grasps all the material as compared to his actual grade performance.

In the process, the teenager can set aside both his self-concept and self-image and review what he is actually doing. Then based on that observation, he can alter his self-image, by now admitting he needs to do more study (altered self - image), which results in better grades (altered self-concept).

I have provided a very simple illustration above. When we look at all the personality attributes which constitute a self-image, the best possible situation would be when the self-image perfectly matches the self-concept. The teenager then knows himself as he is and the results he puts forth match his feelings about himself. The above is true, as long as the teenager sets worthwhile goals and works towards achieving them. Otherwise, this exercise makes no sense. Let me look at an inverse example, where the teenager knows he is lazy and understands others view him as lazy. So what is the big deal about this matching of self-concept and self-image? Really nothing.

By appropriate goal setting, motivation, visualization and hard work, a teenager has the opportunity of crafting his own place under the Sun. So, if he believes he is worthy of achieving a certain outcome in Life and uses the Power of Attraction, among other things to get what he wants, than this Powerful Self Image becomes magnetic in nature. By constant focus on his goals, he now can extend his aura and influence to the world of self-concept. Now everyone around him sees, understands and respects his goals and wishes. You then reach a point where there is a complete match between his self-image (what he sees himself as) and his self-concept (how others see him as a mirror image of what he is). This is the ultimate goal of advanced thinking and living and Success. Match your self-image with your self-concept and you will be super successful in every way.

Another important understanding for a teenager is that he must believe in living his Life from the "inside out". What this means, is that he builds and develops a set of inner core values, which define who he is (self-image). As he strives to achieve this perfect self-image, people around him and outside him come to accept these values to the same degree as he considers valuable (self-concept).

Perfection and alignment of worthwhile goals by creating a self-image and matching this to how the environment views him through a self-concept, is the highest state of teenage development. If the teenager can reach this stage, then his actions are totally accepted, in general, by his environment and the outside world becomes that much more cooperative in this process of reaching his goals.

Positive thinking helps the teenager have the strength and courage to look at his Life plainly; it forces him to step aside and really see who he is with an unbiased acceptance at the present moment, of his strengths and weaknesses. Positive thinking then assists that teenager formulate goals for his Life, which goals are solely unique to him and then gives him the inner motivation to eliminate his negative values--- this helps him build himself up as a new Person, with only positive attributes. Focusing on such values through positive thinking then expands his possibilities as he is able to shoot outwards with his inner core values and perfect the alignment of his dual impressions of self-image and self-concept. With a complete alignment of self-image and self-concept, the teenager is able to garner more strength from his environment and is accepted for what he is and is therefore able to achieve his goals at lightning speed.

Positive thinking brings together the self-image and self-concept, making a teenager that much happier and more Successful in every way possible. Reach out to create this perfection------a World, which honors your wishes and dreams and co-operates in their fulfillment.!!!!!!

CHAPTER 24

POSITIVE THINKING & YOUR CHOICE:
HAPPINESS OR ANXIETY/DEPRESSION

Life is an incredible Blessing!!!!! The teenage years offer the best opportunity to translate this blessing into a really true and virtuous life------ a life based on enjoying all the choices available, in addition to your concerted effort to enjoy what you like doing most. Searching for excellence, the young mind has an incredible opportunity to form good habits and values, which can hold him in good stead through his Lifetime.

Unfortunately, in spite of all these great opportunities, the young teenager today is drifting around with no purpose. With a preoccupation on mundane, nonsensical pursuits like videogames, aimless surfing of the internet, a preoccupation with movies and music, and this teenager is now drifting into a life of no meaning. Do not get me wrong----- there is nothing wrong with playing videogames and surfing the internet; it is just when you do it in the extreme at the expense of other valuable Life exercises that you destroy the very essence of your Being. What happened to teenagers reading at least one new book a week? Or to teenagers volunteering their free time to a good cause, like a charity? Or to youngsters enjoying Sports, playing Chess or whatever they enjoy in an unhindered way? The teenage mind must realize that as he acts, so does the life manifest itself with a specific result. There are two stark choices facing a teenager: the ability to live a life of passion intoxicated with positive thinking or to accept the curse of a Life filled with anxiety, boredom and depression.

Which choice is more valuable to a teenager: naturally one would choose hands down a life of much happiness, fun and fulfillment. A large majority of teenagers do not realize how they live. There is a "herd mentality" and every teenager tries to measure up to the common ideal of the peer group and as a result such teenager attracts Life results, which are devastating. Positive thinking is a choice and a life of happiness, self-fulfillment and fun is the automatic result of that choice. Positive thinking does not exist in a vacuum but in its relationship to other aspects of your Life. When you think positive in terms of your relationship with your values, your Energy use, your cultivation of good habits, your acceptance of honest, hard work then all of these relationships create a dramatic change in your Life result.

What impact does your Lifestyle, your thinking process and your day-to- day action have on your future? It has all the impact one can dream of. If you grow restless and bored of what you are doing, constantly shifting from one videogame to another or one music album to another, this psychological temperament shifts forward to other important aspects of your Life like study and sports. On the other hand, if you practice positive-minded goals and visualize a wonderful and significant life and start practicing and preparing for it now, your Life changes for the better.

My advice to all teenagers is to consider slowing down on all your videogames, the internet and numerous aimless and useless pursuits. Try to focus on what you think might help you long-term.

Set goals, dream big and work hard to get to where you want to be. Think positive and the world will come to your door!!!!!

CHAPTER 25

POSITIVE THINKING & SELF-CONFIDENCE

Self-confidence is a remarkable quality. It moves mountains to get you closer to your dream. And self-confidence results from an inner quality, which trusts your ability to get what you want. That particular image of self-confidence makes you improve your relationships with not only your loved ones, but in addition with your peer group and the world at large. Self-confidence is the spark, which creates the strength and persistence for you to try harder, when hope has failed you in the short-term. And self-confidence blazes a path, where people start believing in your plans and co-operate with you in the fulfillment of such dreams and plans.

How important is self-confidence in its ability to help teenagers reach their dreams faster? For one thing, self-confidence is not an inherited trait. It is something, which needs to be cultivated. And it can be cultivated easily, when a teenager realizes how important this feeling is in achieving results in his day--to-day Life. The teenager has just to look around himself to see the paucity of this trait in individuals surrounding him. When he sees a particular movie or hears a particular song, that trait leaps to the surface. The teenager just feels the surge of energy from an outstanding artiste, presenting his talent to the world. Now, if only the teenager, could cultivate this level of self-confidence???

Unfortunately, it is not so easy to develop this particular quality. Self-confidence is the end result of a lot of other things (first) done well. First, the foundation of good values is a beginning for the teenager; secondly, the practice of good habits in study and sport and thirdly, the respect for others is important. As the teenager starts achieving one goal after another, the self- confidence grows. So the teenager is encouraged to set tangible short-term goals and reward himself for their achievement. Small rewards go a long way into developing self-confidence.

Positive thinking assists you in believing that anything and everything is possible. And if your Mind stays fixated long enough on one idea, then that idea must express itself in your Physical Reality (Law of Attraction). Armed with the belief that you are already self-confident and that you can get anything you wish, you will now attract your wishes on the material plane. And at the same time, your self-confidence will develop dramatically.

Positive thinking, self-confidence, dreaming big, and implementation of the Law of Attraction all go hand-in-hand to make your Life that much more beautiful and worthwhile. You are an artist with a paintbrush and you can paint anything you wish on the canvas of your Life.

CHAPTER 26

POSITIVE THINKING & PERSONAL VALUES/PRINCIPLES

Personal values and principles form the foundation for your Life Action and Purpose. And what better time to lay this foundation, then when you are young? Teenagers have a remarkable capacity to formulate worthwhile goals; their young, active and curious mind helps them understand and adjust to things around them very quickly. This really is the best time to inculcate good values and principles in their life. It does not matter what they do or how they choose to express themselves in their career; if their values are strong, not only will they be successful in what they choose to do, but their impact on the world will be significant.

Some suggested personal values are:

1. I commit to lead an honest and dignified Life.
2. I promise to help others in the fulfillment of their dreams first before I worry about my own interests.
3. I will develop the right quality of hard work to get to where I want to go.
4. I believe in the value of Positive thinking and its role in helping me lead a successful Life, dedicated to serving others.
5. I truly believe in the Power of Attraction and will commit to putting in writing, my goals, plan and purpose in Life.
6. I understand and accept that there is no shortcut to hard work and honesty in achieving my goals and dreams.
7. I believe in being persistent in my effort to achieve my dream.
8. I will never give up and know that if I truly believe in something it must come into fruition in the External World.
9. I deserve a good and worthwhile Life.
10. I will visualize in advance the achievement of my goals and act every moment as if I have already attained my goal.
11. I will stay positive and away from negative energy and influence.
12. I believe in the value of goal-setting and will consistently set reachable goals.
13. I will live my Life with remarkable Enthusiasm and Positive Energy.
14. I believe that the Universal Energy will assist me in the fulfillment of my dreams, wishes and goals.

These are some of the personal values which will serve as a foundation for a successful Life. Teenagers can add or delete from this list, but they must have a list of abiding values, which are preferably in writing.

Positive thinking and personal values make it that much more fun to achieve your Goals , thus making your Life a dream comes true.

CHAPTER 27

POSITIVE THINKING & TIME MANAGEMENT

Time management is such a crucial skill for teenagers; it is totally unbelievable that more teens do not understand nor practice this art. Time management means organizing all your activities in neat tight spots so you can spend your time more wisely and get more from each moment of Life. It also means that you can play more and rest more. It was many years past my teenage Life that I learnt the value of time management. In the meantime, I was like any regular teenager, who had school study and school assignment and sports responsibilities. My weekends were not used very productively since schools were closed then and there was less demand on my time. It was only later on when I arrived in a new country, that I was forced to come to terms with time management demands. I now had to wash my clothes, cook my food, find new friends and do a host of things I had never done in my country of birth.

Time management works best in a concept involving allocating activity in "blocks of time". I have referred to this subject matter earlier in the book. However, I want to go a little deeper into this subject. First a teenager must prioritize his activities. What are the most important things he needs to do on a daily basis? My recommended list would include the following:

1. Attendance at school on a 100% basis.
2. At least two hours of home work and research study daily.
3. At least one hour of quality time with parents and family every day.
4. At least one hour of sports daily.
5. At least two hours of rest and relaxation.
6. Some time devoted to a hobby.

In terms of planning school and college study, an understanding of what your grades are dependent on accompanied with and a greater emphasis on the subjects attracting such higher grade is vital. Also, if you find a certain subject difficult to grasp, then extra time to study this subject should be planned for in your time management schedule. The home work and research study is crucial from a disciplinary point of view and creates some strong values for a teenager, which values will make him perform at the top five per cent of every class. In terms of sport, this is a great distracter and a wonderful physical exercise form. Rest and relaxation are crucial for a young teenager and time must be taken out every day to achieve this outcome. Hobbies are also interesting, and a teenager should be encouraged to explore what he enjoys the most.

Now let us further study the time management model. Once a time model is set on paper, this becomes the official goal for the week. At the end of the week, the teenager must log in to discover what he has accomplished as compared to his time management goal. Has he hit his goals? Has he lagged behind? If he has lagged behind, what is the cause of this? I cannot emphasize more strongly how important it is to follow up on your goals, to ensure you are doing what you need to do to stay on top of the class. Teenagers would be well advised to get the support and ideas of a parent or school counselor in crafting this time management study plan. The teenager must also explore consulting with other experts with a view to improving his performance.

Now how does positive thinking help with time management skills? Because time management, initially, can be an arduous process. Here I am asking a teenager to commit to what subjects he will study in his free time, to what intensity and on which day. Most teenagers are quite haphazard in their study program and usually study a few days or a week before an exam. This is the worst way to study. By forcing a teenager's hand to commit to a regular time schedule, you are creating a massive sense of discipline ---------initially it is hard for a teenager to subject himself to this process. What the teenager must remember is the rewards associated with this action like, doing more work in less time, having more free time, having more fun and being more balanced. It is the rewards which will constantly motivate the teenager to stay on track with time management.

Positive thinking and unflinching courage on the teenager's part assists him in creating realistic goals in terms of study, research, sport, play and hobby and family time. Positive thinking also assists a teenager in being honest with himself when he compares his weekly goal with his actual performance. Positive thinking provides an inspiration and hope to the young teenager to excel in everything he does. It then becomes a plank or support, helping him get to where he wants to go, with respect to study and sports management.

Do not ever underemphasize the need for positive thinking in its relationship to time management study. A smart student, an outstanding sportsman, a good communicator and a happy family Life are all end results of the proper application of Positive thinking.

CHAPTER 28

POSITIVE THINKING & CULTURAL INFLUENCE

A culture in many ways defines us. Ask a person what it means to be an American or a Canadian and a whole host of attributes come to the fore. These include established ways of doing things, conditioned ways of rational thought and a basic value system acceptable to most. It also defines how you dress, how you talk, how you think, how you act, how you eat and a myriad of other things. Every nationality in the World attracts its own definition of Value, Lifestyle and Living Conditions. Why am I talking about cultural influence in this chapter?

Because culture can either help you grow or inhibit you. If a teenager totally identifies himself with a specific culture, then that conditioning causes him to look at other cultures with a "foreign" attitude. What do I mean by "foreign attitude?" Foreign attitude is defined by the uncertainty and accompanying fear of dealing with someone who comes from somewhere else, with a different way of dress and speech and a different background and value system.

Schools and colleges must instill a sense of appreciation of cultural diversity. This sense is very evident in most Canadian schools and colleges. How does it help you to be sensitive to other cultures? It helps you through a common shared understanding that we all belong to one human race, with all the same needs, wishes and desires. The only difference is that some have more than others.

Culture can be a conditioning experience when it is allowed to create differences between people. In this situation, I would encourage all teenagers to travel around the world when they get an opportunity. So volunteer to travel to the developing world. Do a summer or regular study period in college in a foreign country. This experience will teach you how important it is to understand others; it will also provide you an opportunity to extract the best values from every system. For no cultural system is good or bad; every system has its advantages and weaknesses------ your challenge as a teenager is to find the best values and methods from all cultures and incorporate it into your very own special value system. Then you will be better informed, more communicative, more sensitive to others and in general more successful in your Life in all ways.

And success, by the way, is not just defined as having an expensive sports car, a sexy wife, a business and lots of money in the bank. Success, in my book, is defined as being a happy person, having fun and adventure in your life and helping others while you try to build your own special place in the sun.

Positive thinking creates the constant awareness of the commonality of Man. It also gives you the chance to be kind and sensitive to other cultures. Positive thinking is the link which helps you communicate with others ----- it gives you the strength and courage to live and work together cooperatively in the advancement of a World Cause. Because it is only those with the bigger picture of Life who attract true success and happiness. And without Happiness and Love, what is the meaning of Life??????

CHAPTER 29

POSITIVE THINKING
& CULTIVATION OF
INITIATIVE AND LEADERSHIP

Personal initiative and leadership are important cornerstones of good teenage character. These two attributes help a teenager realize his goals faster and give him a solid foundation to develop his future Life.

So what is initiative? It is the courageous use of new ideas and experiments to approach your Life in a novel yet unique way. It is the ability to make independent decisions on what may or may not be good outcomes for a teenager. It also means doing everything with full vigor, enthusiasm and passion.

And what is Leadership? Leadership is an acquired ability to stand ahead of the crowd. It means acting, thinking and demonstrating your Values in such a way that others not only want to emulate you, but also follow your advice, guidance and action. And why is leadership so important? Because as the teenager blooms into full adulthood, he will interact with others either in a job, career or business. If he possesses leadership abilities, then he will grow further in his career as others look up to him and follow his lead.

Positive thinking helps in creating initiative because it helps you in always being hopeful of good change in the future. A positive thinker knows that initiative must be part of his personality make-up and-----he is not afraid to stick his neck out in new ventures or activities. Positive thinking gives him the courage to try new things while ignoring how his peer group may judge him by such action.

And how does positive thinking influence leadership? Positive thinking creates a powerful "aura" around a teenager and blesses him with abundant self-confidence. This same self-confidence attracts the capacity for leadership, which then helps him get to whatever station in Life he chooses to.

Positive thinking and its application to personal initiative and leadership development creates a World class citizen---- a teenager who always takes risks and who attracts others to him due to his great Energy. And a leader gets to enlist the energy of others in a worthwhile cause, which creates great Success for not only him but to all he touches and leads.............

CHAPTER 30

POSITIVE THINKING & SELF-CONTROL

Self-control is a most admirable human quality. It is the spirit of austerity and simplicity, which accompanies one's Life. It is also an awareness system, which guides you from going astray in your Life in the face of negative environmental forces. So, it is very essential for teenagers to understand and implement self-control in their daily Life. But teenagers in developed countries have no idea of what self-control is or how to bring its elements into their Life. Their daily Life is a constant parade of minor and major pleasure events, as they want to experience more and more material things and other creature comforts. Please do not get me wrong. A teenager deserves to enjoy himself. What I am talking about is the total preoccupation and involvement of such teenager in enjoyment and pleasure at the expense of everything else. Is his whole life made for total devotion to the pursuit of pleasure and excitement? If this is how the young teenager views his future, then the effects of such action is truly bad.

The teenage Mind is a new empty book and the teenage years are the best time to inculcate good value. Are parents spending adequate time with their children showing them how to live a more virtuous life? Not really. So, where does the teenage go for learning good values?

As always, the responsibility rests with the teenager to improve his Life. If he lives in a country like India or China, he may get greater parental guidance, but in North America this is generally lacking.

Self-control basically means self-discipline and resultant Life balance. Positive thinking shows the rewards of some austerity in a teenage Life. The rewards of such behavior are a healthy, happy and balanced Life with accumulation of no bad habits like drinking, smoking or drugs.

The application of positive thinking in relationship to self-control creates a better developed teenager, endowed with more self discipline; it assists in the creation of a simpler teenage soul, who enjoys Life but knows everything must be within limits. And positive thinking gives him the courage to stay on his Life track, in spite of negative parental and environmental influence.

CHAPTER 31

POSITIVE THINKING & A PLEASING PERSONALITY

A pleasing personality is another important foundation of teenage character. What do I mean by pleasing personality? It is a teenager who smiles a lot and stays positive in good times and bad. It is a teenager with a good sense of humor. It is a person who likes to help other students when required or inspires fellow students to get involved in sports. It is a natural leader who guides others to believe in their dreams and excel in whatever activities they choose to engage in. It is a person, who others feel privileged and happy to be around.

Is this is a tall order for teenagers? You bet it is. But these qualities can be developed. The rewards for such activity is a more active social life, the opportunity to have more friends, an invitation to more parties and social events and a pride for the family to be blessed with such a wonderful child.

Positive thinking, by its very nature inculcates the beginnings of a pleasing personality. However, a teenager must go beyond positive thinking to create the qualities of a pleasing personality. He must utilize the art of positive thinking as he improves and builds on his other skills like communication, leadership and the spirit of enthusiasm.

Teenagers who acquire a pleasing personality go further, make more friends and influence people greatly. They go up the social and career ladder and one day become captains of industry.

My advice to every teenager is not to take yourself too seriously. Make every day and each moment in Life an adventure. Choose to ignore negativism around you. Laugh at people who try to ridicule you or control you. Keep your eye on the ball. And everything you do, keep the glow of Life alive. Stay positive, happy and continue to be pleasing to everyone. The world will then beat down your door. You will become successful and famous. Who really does not like a pleasing personality??????

CHAPTER 32

POSITIVE THINKING & ACCURATE THOUGHT

Accurate thought is the ability to distinguish between right and wrong. It is the power to separate rational thought from fantasy, to separate thought from irrational emotion. Accurate thought is a great Power, which can help a teenager succeed in his Life.

So how does a teenager develop accurate thought? By being able to understand the differences between rational thought and irrational thinking, by understanding the differences between rational emotion and irrational emotion. It is being able to understand all the conditioning he has been exposed to and the ability to distinguish good from bad, right from wrong. It means being able to identify the various emotions of fear, anxiety, depression, boredom and trying to figure out which emotions are valuable to him and which need to be discarded or at the least ignored.

Positive thinking helps grow accurate thought. Because positive thinking is ultimately responsible for allowing you to get to where you want to go and isolating the qualities you need to get there.

Accurate thought will help a teenager avoid waste of unnecessary emotional energy. It will assist him in collecting and focusing his mental energy in the devotion of his goals and objectives. Aided with positive thinking, accurate thought will clarify goals and provide an effective road map for constant success for the Teenager.

Accurate thought will force the teenager to analyze how he thinks; it will also aid him in seeing the effect of positivism on final Life result versus the impact of being depressed or bored on his Life. Knowing what is of greatest value to him, he will learn not to associate with depressing thoughts or boredom but deflect his energy in the direction of his dreams. Staying positive all the time, aided with the application of accurate thought will get the teenager to move mountains.

CHAPTER 33

SUMMARY

This book attempts to explain the relationship between Positive Thinking and the 32 challenging aspects of teenage Life. The author recommends that when you read this book, you pay particularly close attention to these 32 challenging Life issues. Once you understand the importance of these 32 areas, then you can employ positive thinking to help you overcome any obstacles encountered in fulfillment goals in these areas. These issues are not in any order of significance. Mastery of these 32 challenges is most important for a teenager's successful growth and development. These are your special challenges:

1. Success
2. Sex
3. Health, Sports and Physical Activity
4. Family Environment
5. Religion, Faith and Conditioning
6. Study
7. Meditation and Yoga
8. Stress Management
9. Peer Pressure
10. Role of Public Speaking
11. Dealing with Change
12. Puberty-----Dealing with immaturity
13. Love
14. Money Savings Habits
15. Competition
16. Creative Imagination
17. Law of Attraction
18. Career, Skill and Talent search
19. Future Career Choices
20. Success and Entrepreneurship
21. Goal Setting and Visualization
22. Motivation and Role Models
23. Self Concept versus Self Image
24. Happiness versus Anxiety/Depression
25. Self-Confidence
26. Personal Values
27. Time Management
28. Cultural Influences
29. Cultivation of Initiative and Leadership
30. Cultivating Self-Control
31. Cultivating a Pleasing Personality
32. Cultivating Accurate Thought

These 32 areas are the most vital areas affecting teenagers. A chapter is devoted to each of these important areas and the role of positive thinking in relationship to this challenge is expounded.

The author hopes that the teenager develops more enthusiasm, passion and intention in achieving his goals. This teenager has the power to have more fun, more effectiveness, and makes more friends while leading an exemplary life.

It is the author's hope and fervent prayer that reading this book and implementing the ideas therein assist in developing a more rounded, well balanced teenager, who is willing to take the responsibility for his Life. The author also prays that an intelligent teenager can, by employing the principles and values outlined in this book, create results which are Earth-defying.

My sincere wishes, to you teenager, wherever you live in the world. You were Born to Win!!!!

Do believe that you can do anything you set your mind to do and that you have the ability to surmount all obstacles which come in your way. Positive thinking will help you in your quest to be a giant in your chosen field of endeavor and help you have better relationships and achieve the final and most desirable result-----a sense of self-satisfaction and happiness as you serve others quintessentially.